Chinese Sculpture

Zhao Wenbing provides an accessible, illustrated introduction to the sculptural art of China, including the magnificent Terracotta Army, Buddhist sculpture, tomb carvings, architectural sculpture, exchange with foreign cultures and Chinese sculpture today. *Chinese Sculpture* takes the reader through the unique aesthetic features of sculpture in China, arguing that the evolution of this sculpture parallels the development of Chinese culture through history.

Introductions to Chinese Culture

The thirty volumes in the Introductions to Chinese Culture series provide accessible overviews of particular aspects of Chinese culture written by a noted expert in the field concerned. The topics covered range from architecture to archaeology, from mythology and music to martial arts. Each volume is lavishly illustrated in full color and will appeal to students requiring an introductory survey of the subject, as well as to more general readers.

Zhao Wenbing

CHINESE SCULPTURE

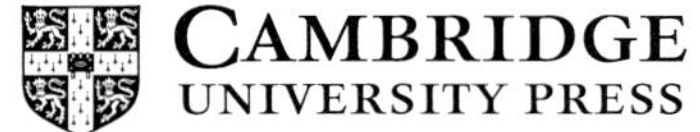

CAMBRIDGE UNIVERSITY PRESS
Cambridge, New York, Melbourne, Madrid, Cape Town,
Singapore, São Paulo, Delhi, Tokyo, Mexico City

Cambridge University Press
The Edinburgh Building, Cambridge CB2 8RU, UK

Published in the United States of America by Cambridge University Press,
New York

www.cambridge.org
Information on this title: www.cambridge.org/9780521186773

Originally published by China Intercontinental Press as
Chinese Sculpting (9787508513270) in 2010

This updated edition is published by Cambridge University Press
with the permission of China Intercontinental Press under
the China Book International programme .

For more information on the China Book International programme, please visit
http://www.cbi.gov.cn/wisework/content/10005.html

First published 2012

Printed and bound in China by C&C Offset Printing Co., Ltd

A catalogue record for this publication is available from the British Library

ISBN 978-0-521-18677-3 Paperback

Contents

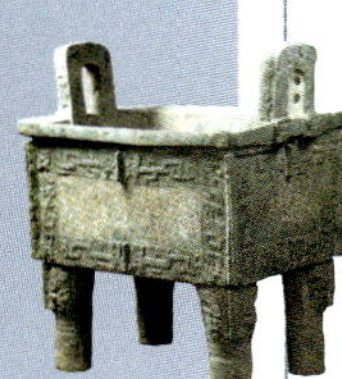

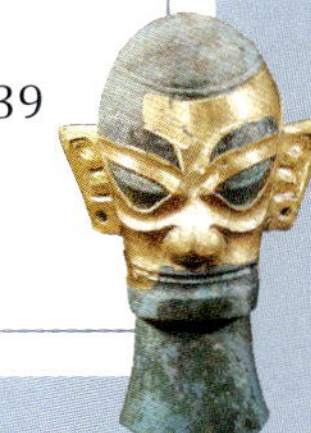

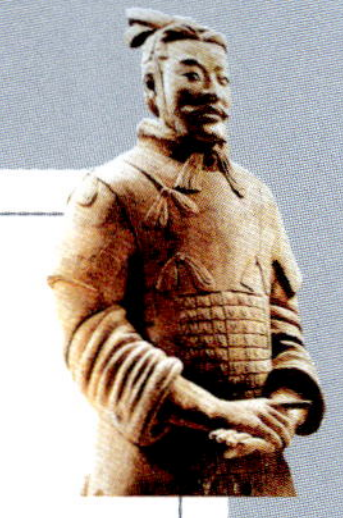

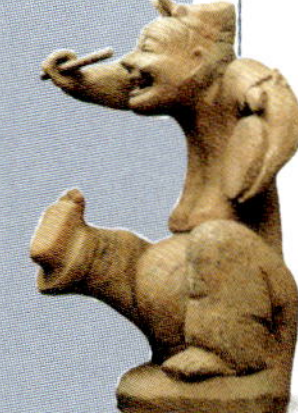

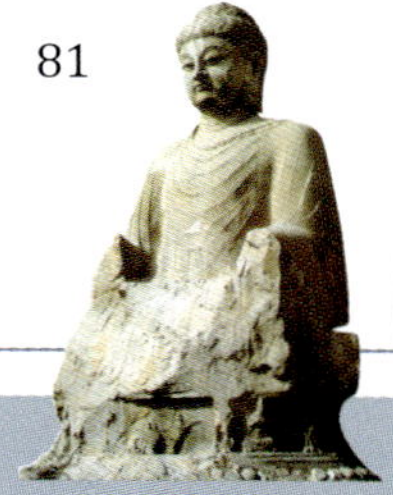

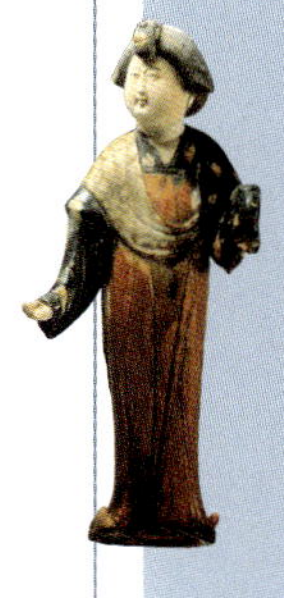

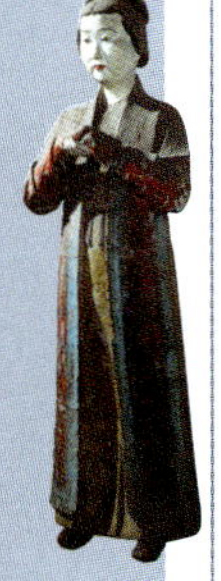

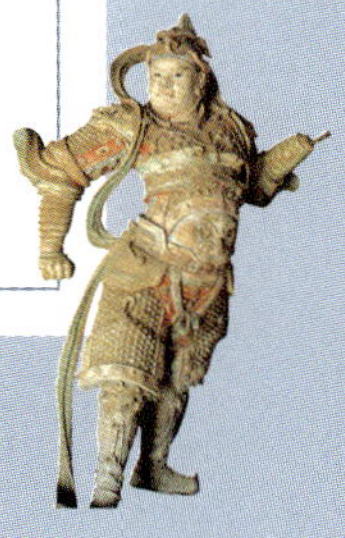

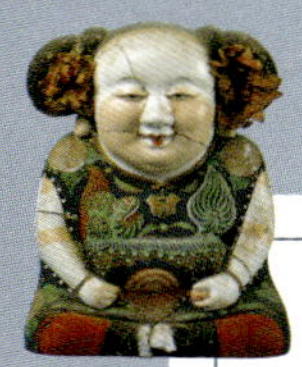

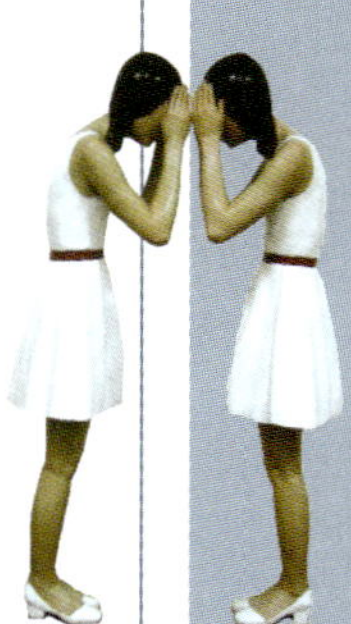

Foreword

Emerging from one of the oldest civilizations, Chinese sculpture has thrived for thousand of years. Through time and cultural developments, Chinese sculpture has taken different paths in different regions and cannot be easily categorized. It develops as times change and culture evolves.

The development of sculpture is often closely allied to historical context. The life of sculptural arts is typically bound with the prosperity of a country.

Take Chinese sculpture as an example. Sculptures characterized by stateliness and ritualism emerged during the Shang and Zhou dynasties (1600–221 BC); pieces full of majesty and cohesion surfaced during the Han (206 BC–AD 220) and Tang (618–907) dynasties; the Wei, Jin and Northern and Southern dynasties (265–589) produced Buddhist images full of religious influence and spirituality; pieces from the Song Dynasty (960–1279) are exquisite and moderate; while the Ming and Qing dynasties (1368–1911) produced colorful, secular sculptures.

Chinese sculptural art first emerged in the Neolithic Age (10,000–4000 BC). The simplest sculptures correlate closely with early witchcraft, such as stone arrangements and clay and pottery sculptures representing women found in the graves of primitive man. They suggest a relationship between sculpture and the beliefs of primitive man. They were generally made of clay, jade or stone and their form combines human-shaped figures and practical wares. These sculptures displayed the primary nonrepresentational characteristics of Chinese sculpture.

Bronze casting techniques gradually replaced pottery techniques. Similar to primitive society, the sculptural arts of

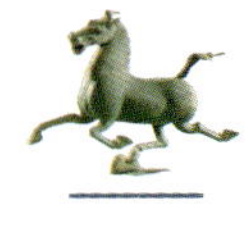

the Zhou Dynasty (1046–256 BC) began to take shape. Works from this era are rare. Bronze sculptures were mainly used to strengthen spiritual beliefs during the Shang and Zhou dynasties, when belief in spirits and deities and compliance with a ritualistic system were popular. Ferocious and formidable bronze sculptures from the Shang and Zhou dynasties generate a sense of intimidation. Artistically, the most important achievement was the highly ornamental patterns on such sculptures, reflecting exquisite bronze casting and their unique expression of Chinese characters.

The idea of China as a universal underlying imperial concept began during the Qin Dynasty (221–206 BC), which produced breathtakingly brilliant sculpture. The most significant achievement is the Terracotta Warriors and Horses in the Mausoleum of Emperor Shihuang. The magnificent sculptures have a lot of character, fully displaying unique Chinese techniques and the ambition of the Qin Dynasty.

Following the development of excellent techniques during the Qin Dynasty, sculptural arts of the Han Dynasty show new styles and themes—the romance and humanity of the culture of the Chu Kingdom and the grand features of the culture of the ancient northern people. The former style is mainly demonstrated by pottery sculptures such as the "Woman Dancer" and the "Story Teller." The latter is shown on large stone sculptures including the stone carvings in front of the Tomb of Huo Qubing.

Buddhism was introduced to China from India during the Eastern Han Dynasty (25–220) and became popular among both emperors and common people during the Wei and Jin dynasties (265–420) due to the prosperity of metaphysics and the loss of influence of Confucianism and Taoism. The development of the religion led to an increasing number of Buddhist images, a factor that was also influenced by social unrest, regime change

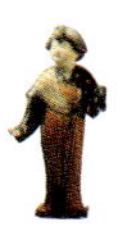

and poor standards of living during the Northern and Southern Dynasties (420–589). Large works in grottoes and the construction of Buddhist temples took Chinese sculpture into a new and important stage. The Buddhist statues in the Gandhāra style were prevalent in the early stage of Chinese sculpture, which was influenced directly by Buddhist statues in India. Before long, local Chinese culture adopted similar styles and Buddhist statues with Chinese characteristics emerged gradually.

Grotto construction started during the fourth century and thrived between the fifth and the eighth centuries (between the Wei and Jin dynasties and the Tang Dynasty). The quantity and scale of the Buddhist statues grew despite a movement to exterminate Buddhism during that period. After the eighth century, enthusiasm for grottoes started ebbing away as culture evolved, regimes changed and temple construction thrived. Many of the grottoes and Buddhist statues still in evidence today were made between the fourth and eighth centuries. The Mogao Grottoes in Dunhuang (Gansu), Maijishan Grottoes in Gansu, Yungang Grottoes in Datong (Shanxi) and Longman Grottoes in Luoyang represent the key sculptural styles of the time. Such grottoes preserve the evolving styles and characteristics of Chinese sculpture between the Wei and Jin dynasties and the Tang Dynasty.

As time progressed, Buddhism became more integrated with Chinese culture and beliefs. There has been reciprocal influence between Buddhism, Taoism and Confucianism. The colored sculptures in the Jin Temple (Shanxi) and Dazu Stone Carving in Sichuan fully embody the combination of Buddhism, Taoism and Confucianism. It was from this time that Buddhist statues displayed a calmness and maturity, reflecting a combination of various kinds of culture.

Besides a belief in Buddhism, emperors of various dynasties also attached great importance to the construction of their tombs.

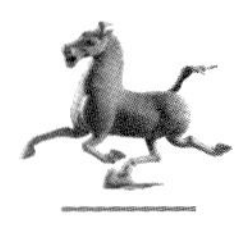

Many important sculptures outside tombs have been found since the Western Han Dynasty (206 BC–AD 25). The basic forms of tombs were well established by the Wei and Jin dynasties. The scale of tombs reached a peak during the Sui and Tang dynasties (581–907). Some sculptures evoked auspicious animals that could protect people against evil spirits, such as stone beasts, *tianlu* (an animal with a single horn) and *bixie* (which has two horns). These became symbols of dynamic spirits and were placed in imperial tombs after the Wei and Jin dynasties.

The pottery tomb figurine is also a profound part of Chinese sculpture. Various pottery tomb sculptures and sculptural beasts—from the terracotta warriors and houses of the Qin and Han dynasties to the tri-color glazed pottery of the Tang Dynasty—embody the characteristics of their times, such as the elegant and clear appearance of Wei and Jin Period pieces and the plump beauty of pieces from the Tang Dynasty.

Chinese sculpture began to decline during the Ming and Qing dynasties. Generally speaking, even religious sculptures became mediocre. In spite of this, some great masterpieces appeared, especially painted clay sculptures. The Shuanglin Temple in Pingyao and the Qiongzhu Temple in Kunming have in their collections some of the most brilliant clay sculptures from the Ming and Qing dynasties. The Shuanglin Temple is famous for the Guanyin and Weituo statues and more than 2,000 vivid figures. The Qiongzhu Temple is known for the 500 Arhat statues, a perfect combination of religious and secular art. The development of painted clay sculptures was connected to prosperity in arts and crafts during the Ming and Qing dynasties.

As one of the key art categories, classical architecture is closely related to the sculptural arts. Architectural styles and art forms changed a lot from the Qin and Han dynasties to the Ming and Qing dynasties. Although the splendid palaces of the Qin and

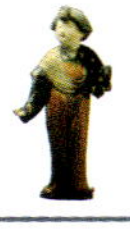

Han dynasties have turned to ashes, surviving eaves tiles and large hollow bricks still display the power of the mighty Qin. Eaves tiles decorated with four patterns associated with four deities and Chinese characters, along with stone sculptures are representative sculptural achievements of the Han Dynasty and define the stylistic progress of Chinese sculpture.

The architectural sculpture on palaces from the Sui and Tang dynasties show the cultural inclusion and confidence of the times. The Great Wild Goose Pagoda in Xi'an, a well-preserved Buddhist pagoda, is truly the best of the line-carving works from the Tang Dynasty. Architectural sculpture during the Yuan Dynasty (1206–1368) is a mirror of culture and the national strength of the times. Sculptures often have strong outlines but lack spirit and cohesion. Architectural relics from the Ming and Qin are profound. The Imperial Palace in Beijing represents the level of achievement of architectural sculpture. It pays equal attention to ornamental and practical functions and is even more exquisite than examples from previous dynasties.

Sculptural examples from folk architecture are also very important and mainly include brick sculptures and woodcarvings, which are close to folk culture. The smart *Muhura* and simple "Big Afu" are full of the vitality of folk life.

Entering the twentieth century, traditional religious sculpture was in a stage of decline in China. Although small-sized folk sculpture was still flourishing, it failed to become mainstream. Since the Xinhai Revolution (1911), the art of Chinese sculpture has experienced distinctive changes and development. The introduction of the Western style of sculpture was accepted by some fine arts schools. The European classic and academic idea of sculpture gradually grew in China. From around the May 4th Movement in 1919 to the 1930s, more young people went to learn sculpture in the West. After these people returned home,

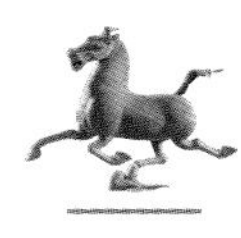

most were engaged in arts education. Their efforts promoted the development of modern sculpture in China.

After the establishment of the People's Republic of China in 1949, great changes have taken place in sculptural art. Different fine arts colleges and universities set up sculpture departments and sent students to study in the Soviet Union. Between the 1940s and 1970s, there appeared serial sculptural works that were full of revolutionary passion and Soviet influence. These works not only represented great changes in the way of sculpting, but, more importantly, their changes in form reflected the formation of new political values. To date, China's modern sculpture demonstrates a variety of schools and concepts, reflecting a pluralistic society and culture.

Chinese sculptural arts have developed their own style over time and have managed to display aesthetic features and cultural concepts unique to ancient China. The development of Chinese sculpture parallels the history of ancient Chinese culture and aesthetics. It is a visible witness to cultural fusion and exchanges between Han Chinese and other Chinese peoples as well as between China and foreign cultures.

Beginnings of Chinese Sculpture

Pottery and Jade Sculptures in Primitive Times

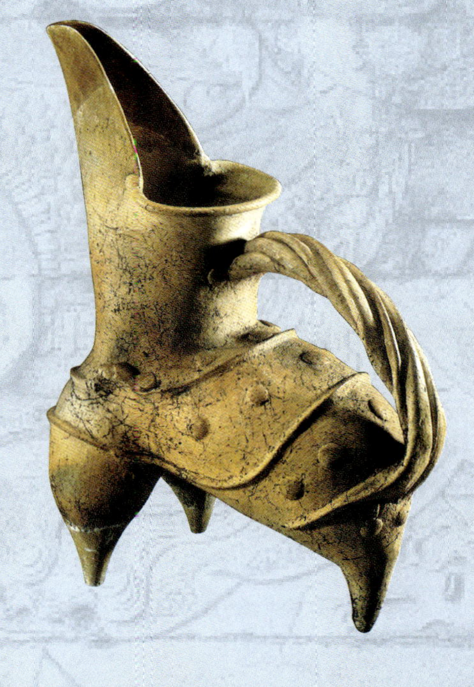

Chinese sculpture is one of the oldest art forms in the world. The oldest examples date back to the Neolithic Age. During the 1990s, an 8,000-year-old stone sculpture of a dragon, which is around 20m in length, was unearthed. It is believed to be the earliest large stone sculpture ever discovered in China.

Chinese pottery sculptures first peaked during the Neolithic Age. By this time, people had mastered potting techniques. Most sculptures from that time are made from pottery, wood, stone or bone and represent human and animal forms. Surviving sculptures are mostly made from pottery or jade. As with those of other early civilizations, these vivid sculptures were made mainly to meet the needs of primitive religion and hunting, but they clearly display the early abstract characteristics of China's formative arts. Our knowledge of this period is based largely on archaeological finds. Each discovery helps us to understand ancient civilization and sculpture better.

Pottery sculptures in primitive times

Primitive pottery sculptures were made soon after the emergence of potting techniques. They had mostly practical functions. The "pottery pot" is most common. It is often designed with a human face or human head at the top, or shaped like an animal. In fact, such designs are also very common in other early cultures, such as ancient Persia and India. In ancient China, pottery sculptures fell into one of three types: animal shapes; circular or relief sculptural ornaments with animal or human form as part of an article (such

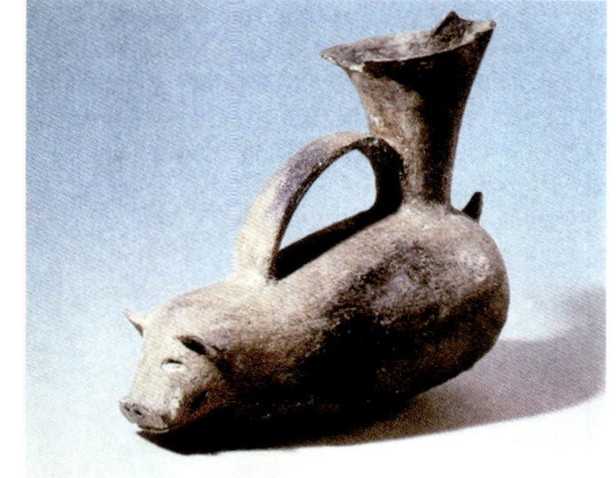

Pottery boar-shaped cooker, the Neolithic Age.

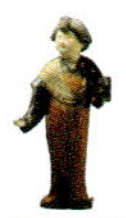

as a cover, knob or surface); and single animal or portrait sculptures such as nude female sculptures or hand-shaped sculptures. The last usually had obvious primitive religious features.

Pottery figure sculptures

Famous Neolithic Chinese pottery includes pieces from the Yangshao, Majiayao and Dawenkou cultures. Many excellent ornamental sculptures have been well preserved, including a lively 12.5cm pottery piece of a maiden's head unearthed in Gaositou, Lixian County, Gansu Province. It is made of orange yellow clay by means of simple techniques. It belongs to the Banshan branch of the *Yangshao* culture and it is often mentioned in university courses on the history of Chinese arts. The features of the face are simple, with three hollow ovals representing the eyes and mouth. Her ears and nose are also simple. Her face is relaxed and full of pleasure. The sculpture gives the impression of sincerity and simplicity.

***Yangshao* culture**
Yangshao culture (5000 BC–3000 BC), one of the key examples of matriarchal society in China, was first found in *Yangshao* Village, Mianchi County, Henan Province, hence the name "*Yangshao* culture." The culture left behind some pottery decorated with dark red or black patterns on orange-red or red-brown backgrounds. These are outstanding examples of painted pottery in China's Neolithic period. As a result, it is also known as the "Painted Pottery Culture."

At the top of her head there are thin ornamental ribbons similar to plaits, which reflect the habits of early people. The head is not an independent sculpture work. It is cleverly done, with circular carving as part of the mouth.

Pottery maiden's head, the Neolithic Age.

The unique quality of pottery designed with the sculpted figure of a human head is visible on another masterpiece of Banshan type in *Yangshao*

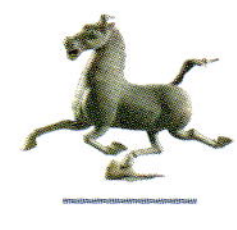

culture, which is a pot with a mouth in the form of a head. The pot was unearthed in Luonan, Shaanxi. It is a well-preserved 23cm pot of red clay with a sculpture of a human head. The eyes and mouth are also hollow holes. The hollows leave behind some shadows that enhance the expressive forces of the sculpture and produce an open feeling of "enlightenment" and "ventilation" bringing the sculpture to life.

The *Yangshao* culture left behind many similar works. The sculpture of a human face unearthed in Chajiaping, Tianshui City, Ganshu, was also originally the top of a mutilated piece of pottery. The life-size female face is part of a large 25.5cm high and 16cm wide article. She has a narrow and flat forehead, beautifully thin, long eyebrows and eyes, reflecting oriental beauty. Her eyes are small and her nose is straight. Her cheekbones are prominent and her face wide. She is smiling, with her lips slightly parted. She is a typical feminine Asian image. This type of sculpture, with apparent sexual features, was probably linked to popular goddess worship. Such worship was full of the warmth of living and the pleasures of life. The sculpture is very different from the religious images that surfaced during later society. These ferocious and intimidating images are discussed in the following chapter.

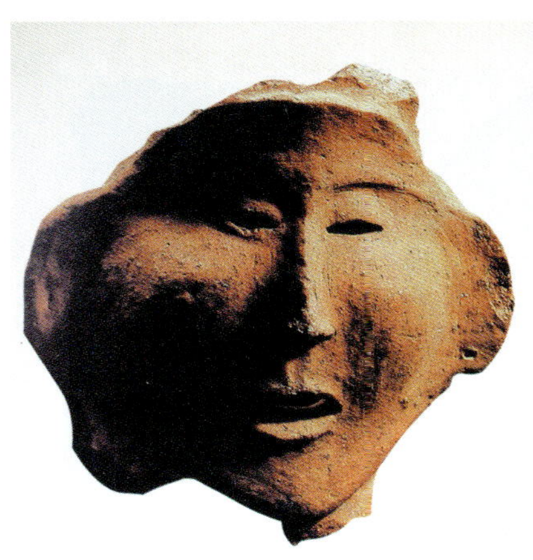

Pottery human face, the Neolithic Age.

Some primitive pottery has colorful paint. Typical examples are pieces combining portraits and sculpture with beautiful patterns. The black patterns on the cover of a piece of Banshan-type

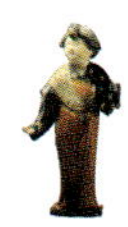

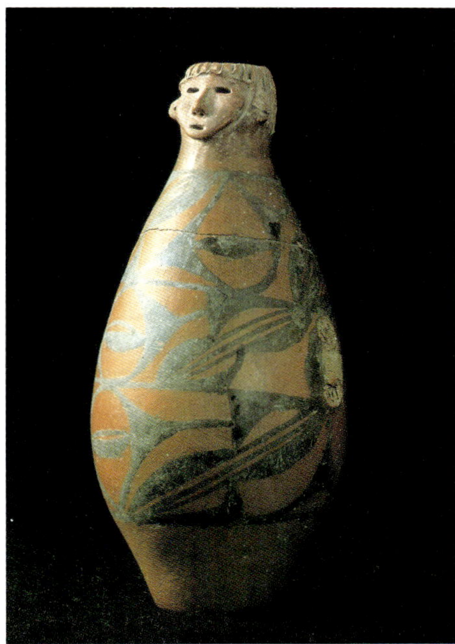
Pottery vase with a colored human head, the Neolithic Age.

human head pottery reflect the techniques, social customs and aesthetic standard of primitive times. The design patterns represent the abstract ornamental features of Neolithic painted pottery. A classic example is a vase unearthed in the Dadiwan Neolithic site in Qinan County, Gansu Province in 1973. It is a human head-shaped painted pottery vase of the Miaodigou type. It is not only well preserved but also beautiful in shape and decoration.

Remarkably, these works not only accurately express the position and proportions of the features of a face but also produce some unique expressions. They are, without doubt, the origins of formative arts, even if the techniques are coarse.

An important archaeological discovery was made in the early 1980s. This was a piece of painted pottery from the Hongshan culture and a piece of painted pottery from a goddess figure. After 1979, archaeologists started large-scale excavations of the Hongshan culture in western Liaoning Province. The temple, the large altar and stone graves were discovered gradually. Radiocarbon dating puts those relics at more than 5,000 years of age. A batch of small pottery figurines of pregnant women was unearthed in the Hongshan culture site in 1982. The proportions

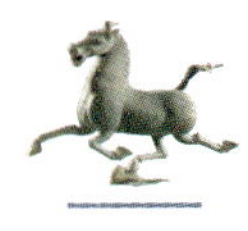

and physiological features of the pregnant women are accurate. Although the head and feet of one piece are mutilated, the body and legs show the craftsman's capability. The protruding abdomen and slightly bent knees in particular make a deep impression. This figurine is suggestive of the "Venus of Willendorf" unearthed in Austria. Relatively speaking, figurines of pregnant women from the Hongshan culture are simple in expression and technique. Regardless of whether they come from the Western or Eastern worlds, statues of pregnant women are closely connected to fertility rituals. Another important masterpiece of the Hongshan culture is a clay sculpture known as "Goddess Head Sculpture." The life-size sculpture is 22.5cm in height and vivid in shape. The features of the face are clear, especially the bright and piercing eyes. This sculpture is full of mystic religious content.

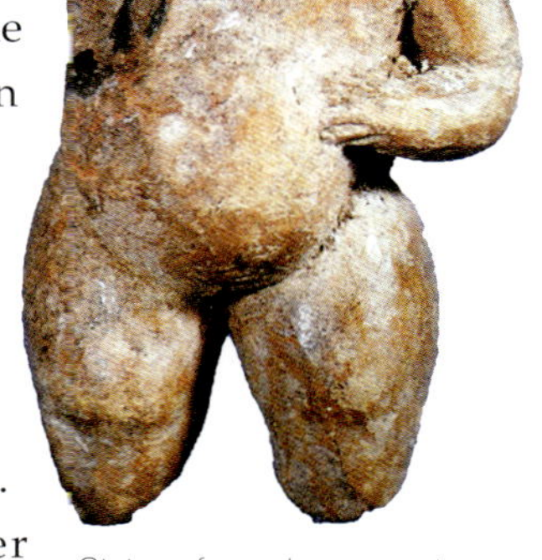

Statue of a nude pregnant woman, the Neolithic Age.

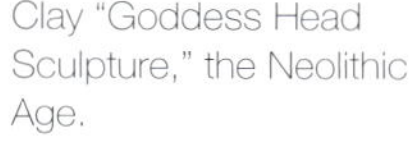

Clay "Goddess Head Sculpture," the Neolithic Age.

Pottery animal sculptures

Animal images are another key subject of primitive sculptures. This includes images of pigs, dogs, sheep, birds and fish. They are widely used in the Hemudu culture in Zhejiang Province. Such animals were common in everyday life. The sculptures are simple in technique and give an impression of simplicity and intelligence.

Some of these sculptures are not static but have a dynamic beauty of movement. Such techniques are not very practical

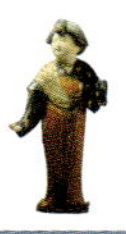

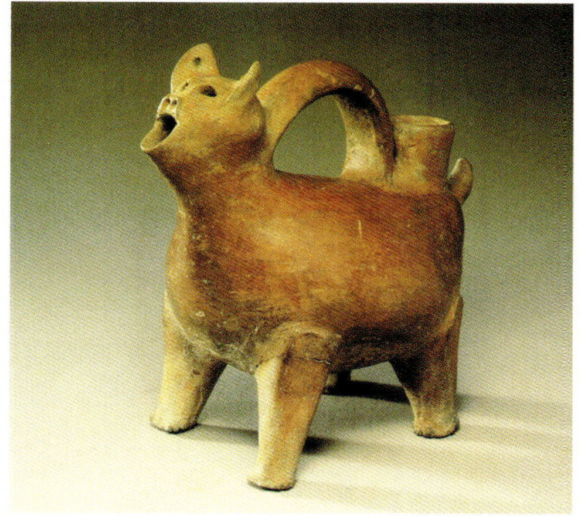

Pottery beast-shaped pot, the Neolithic Age.

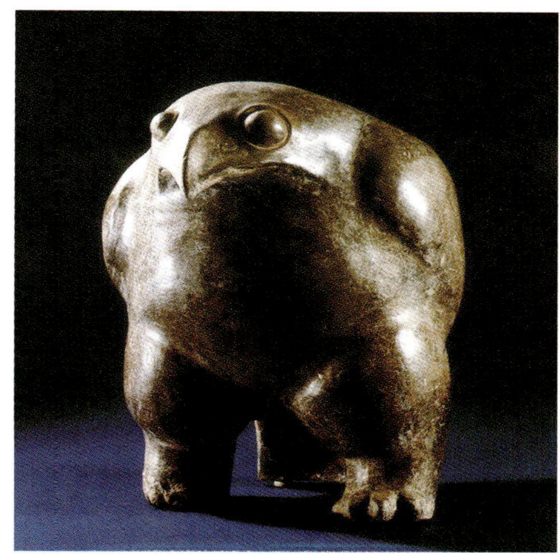

Pottery eagle-shaped *zun* (goblet), the Neolithic Age.

and the sculptures are very vivid. It matches the rules of ancient Chinese formative arts, which lasted for several thousand years. These rules regard "vividness" and "impressionistic style" as the highest standard, above the faithful reproduction of shapes.

The animal shapes are often combined with various practical articles. For example, an eagle-shaped *zun* (a wine vessel), unearthed from a tomb of a mature woman in Taipingzhuang, Huaxian County, Shaanxi Province, belongs to the later works of the Miaodigou type. The shape of the eagle is simple but solid. Its awe-inspiring look is overwhelming from all aspects.

Although some pottery wares are not made in imitation of animal images, people often associate them with them. For instance, a piece of three-foot pottery *gui* belonging to the Longshan culture. Although not in imitation of any animal, it is suggestive

Pottery pot, the Neolithic Age.

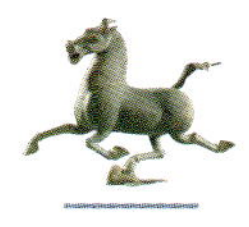

of birds with their heads turned upward. These pieces are rich in abstract features and embody great creativity.

According to a relatively recent archeological discovery, the earliest piece of Chinese sculpture is an 8,000-year-old dragon-shaped stone sculpture. The dragon is around 20m in length. It was unearthed during the 1990s (see *China Cultural Relics News*, 19 March 1995). As an art form, stone sculpture is primitive and religious art form. Besides shapes made from piles of stones, there are also sculptures made of arrangements of shells. For example, dragon and tiger-shaped shell arrangements were unearthed in 1987 on both sides of a dead person for whom the tomb was built in Xishuipo, Puyang, Henan Province. The life-size shell arrangements belong to the *Yangshao* culture and show the majesty and power of the dead man.

Jade sculptures in primitive times

Since primitive times, the Chinese have enriched their aesthetic experience of beauty using jade. Jade attracts people's attention with its excellent quality and its unique features. The qualities of jade were gradually combined with various shapes. People first developed an understanding of circle and square shapes while creating jade articles. They then started experimenting with lines as understanding of shape and outlines grew. The use of curves, in particular, is unique to primitive jade articles.

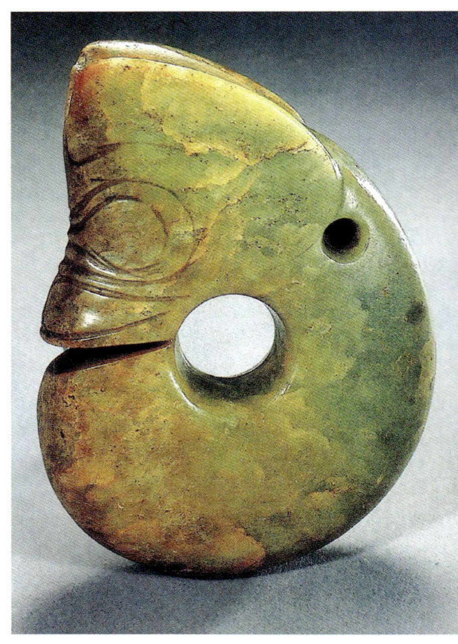

Jade dragon, the Neolithic Age.

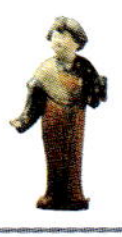

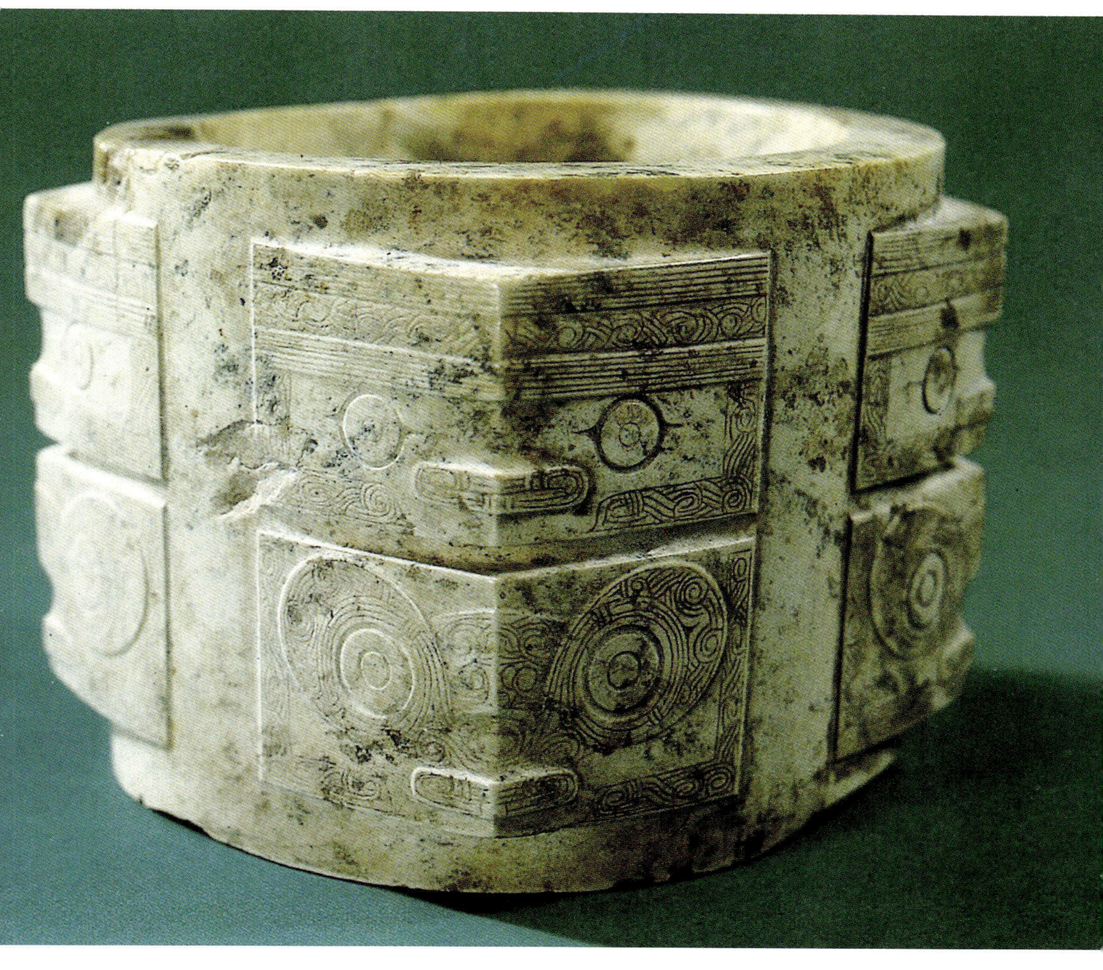

Beast-face pattern *cong* (a cubic article with a round hole in center), the Neolithic Age.

Chinese jade sculptures deal with religion, politics, utility and even morality. The first artistic peak of Chinese jade sculpture emerged in primitive times and was demonstrated by the Hongshan, Liangzhu, Dawenkou and Longshan cultures. The Hongshan culture is particularly worthy of mention. Some simple and abstract dragon-shaped jade sculptures from the

Hongshan culture are suggestive of the imagination of primitive sculptors and their brilliant capacity to abstract. There are also some human faces made of jade with holes at the top through which to run a cord to be used as amulets.

Many jade articles have been unearthed from the Liangzhu culture site dating back about 4,000 years in Jiangsu and Zhejiang provinces. Among them is a jade *cong* (a cubic article with a round hole in center) and jade cicada with animal-face patterns. Another example is a piece of unearthed jade *cong* designed with animal-face patterns on all sides with each line between 0.1–0.2 mm in thickness.

Mature images of animal faces show the cultural features of the Shang and Zhou dynasties and illustrate their heritage and development.

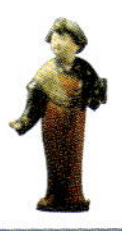

Ferocious Beauty of the Central Plains Civilization

Animal Sculptures in Bronze from the Shang and Zhou dynasties

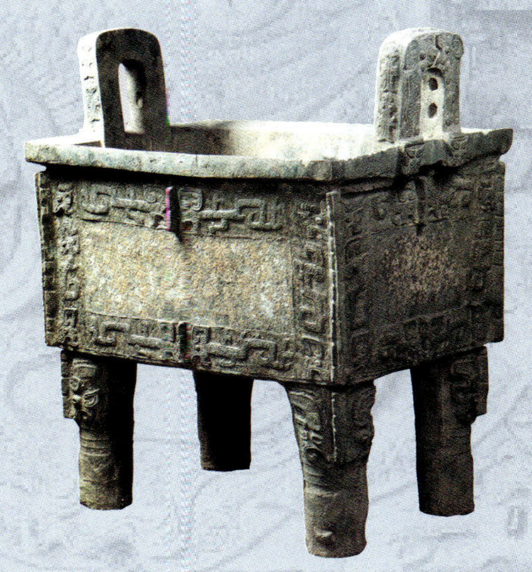

As bronze casting techniques and the ritual culture of the central plains evolved, bronzes from the Shang and Zhou dynasties became more impressive in their technique. Those ferocious and unreal animal images embody the spiritual beliefs of the times. Elaborately decorated patterns fully display exquisite bronze casting techniques and unique shape expression. The sculptural techniques and the highly abstract and organized patterns of the bronzes also influenced jade sculpture.

China entered into the Bronze Age during the Shang Dynasty, around the sixteenth century BC. Ancient formative arts changed very obviously at that time. The artistic shapes and tendencies of each stage are closely associated with the culture of the times.

Generally speaking, the Shang and Zhou period consists of three states including the Shang Dynasty (1600–1046 BC), the Western Zhou Dynasty (1046–771 BC) and the Eastern Zhou Dynasty (770–256 BC). The Eastern Zhou Dynasty is usually divided into the Spring and Autumn Period (770–476 BC) and the Warring States Period (475–221 BC). Though similar, the cultural features of each stage have differences. The differences on the bronzes reflect these different cultural features. The Shang and Zhou dynasties exerted great influence in the ritual system.

Strictly speaking, the Shang and Zhou Period did not produce any independent bronze sculptures. Most sculptures combine vessels and various images. In spite of this, bronze sculptures for sacrificial purposes still make a strong impression and demonstrate intelligence and aesthetic skill in shapes, patterns and functions.

Shang: Magnificent ferocity

During the Shang Dynasty priority was given to religious concepts. People believed in ghosts and deities and had a respect for military aggression. Drinking was very popular. *The Book*

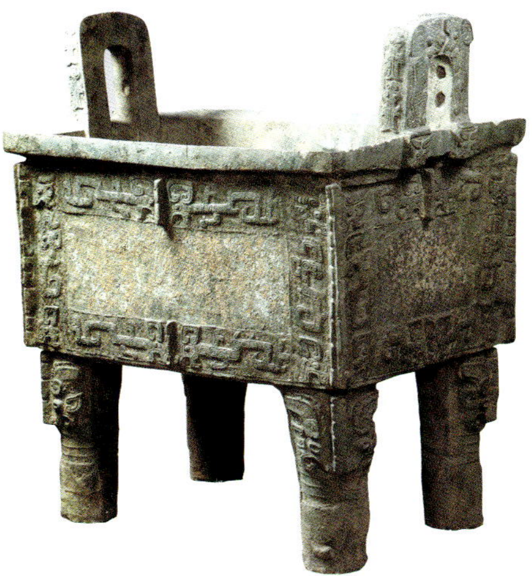
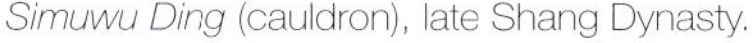

Simuwu Ding (cauldron), late Shang Dynasty.

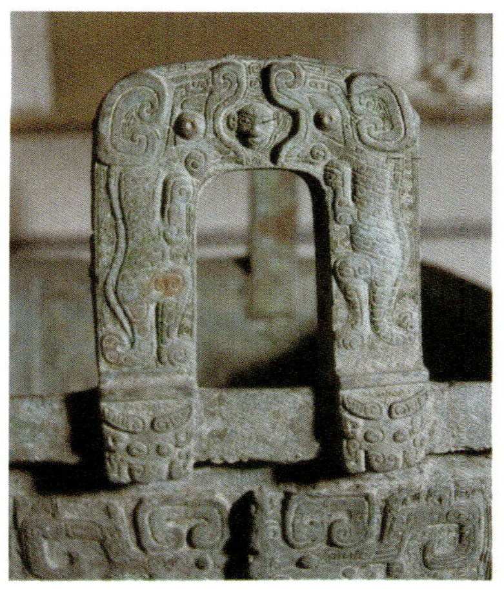

An ear of a Ding.

of Rites said, "Shang people respect deities and offer sacrifices to deities. People pay higher respect to ghosts than rituals, punishments than rewards."

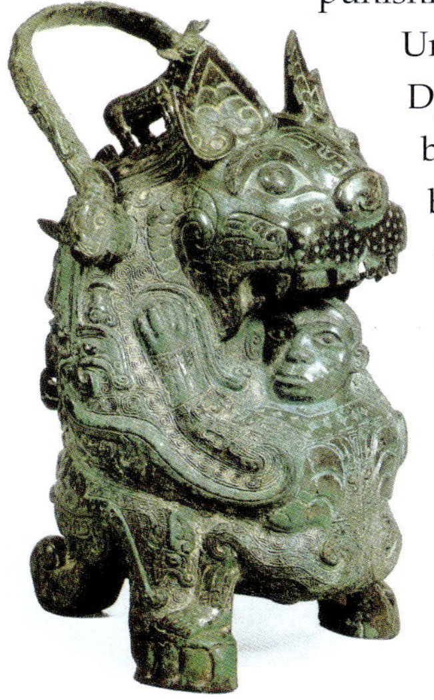

Ehuchiren You, a kind of wine container resembling a snarling tiger devouring a man, late Shang Dynasty.

Under this social influence, the bronzes from the Zhou Dynasty embody the mysterious and majestic. Most bronzes were made for religious rituals, as reflected by their shapes and patterns. The bronze casting techniques reached their peak during the mid- and late Shang Dynasty. Many new works of sculpture emerged and they paid little attention to practical functions. Most works are images of people or mythical animals and give a feeling of intimidation.

The largest and best-preserved heavy bronze ware from the Shang Dynasty is the *Simuwu Ding*, which has a disturbing pattern. Outside of its two handles there is a pair of relief tigers with human heads inside their opening mouths. This pattern is also found in other Shang bronzes. The *Ehushiren*

You (a kind of wine container resembling a snarling tiger devouring a man) is on the verge of being a three-dimensional sculpture, but it is a vessel rather than a sculpture. It is made with typical bronze-casting features from the Shang Dynasty and features fine patterns on the bodies of the tiger and man. The use of complicated background patterns is one of the key features of Shang sculptures.

The main achievements of Shang bronze arts are demonstrated by large numbers of bronze wares in imitation of various animals, including *zun*, *gong*, *you* and other animal-shaped vessels for wine. The animals are mainly rhinoceros, elephant, sheep, tiger and owl.

The most common animal image on bird and beast-shaped *zun* is the owl. According to the *Chou Rituals*, bird and beast-shaped *zun* were widely used for the different sacrificial activities in different seasons by the noble family. As altar wares, they are full of dignified and noble beauty. The casting techniques are exquisite and congruous with social functions. Therefore, such bird and beast-shaped *zun* do not belong to ordinary sculpture, while animal images were not created for aesthetic purposes. The images and the wares were types of tools for communicating with ghosts and deities.

There were rules on the creation of such animal images during the Shang Dynasty. Some patterns, including *taotie* (a beast-like face), *kui* dragon (one-legged monster), phoenix, elephant and tiger,

Taotie

Taotie, one of the ancient mythological beasts in China, is known for having eaten too much. In fact, it died from overeating, and became a symbol of greed. The legend of *Taotie* teaches us that we should be temperate when doing things or asking for something. Nowadays, the Chinese also use *taotie* to describe gluttonous or greedy people. The pattern, also known as the "beast face pattern" was popular on bronze ware from the Shang to the early Western Zhou dynasties.

Elephant-shaped *zun*, late Shang Dynasty.

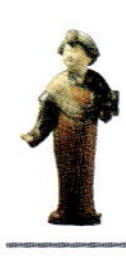

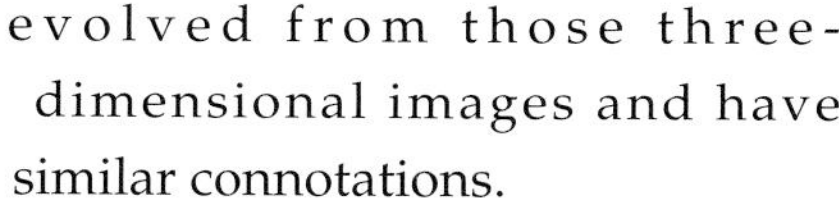

Four-ram square *zun*, late Shang Dynasty.

evolved from those three-dimensional images and have similar connotations.

There were two common bronze casting techniques for bird and beast-shaped *zun*. The first was to combine the images of bird and beast with one piece of bronze ware, such as the four-foot *Simuxin Hu* from the Tomb of Fuhao. The *Simuxin Hu* imitates a beast in the front, a bird at the end, *kui* and tiger on both sides and a long dragon on the cover. The second is to integrate various animal images together, such as a bird head with animal horns and dragon or snake-shaped wings.

There are two typical animal-shaped sculptures surviving from the Shang period. One is the elegant Elephant *zun* from Liling County, Hunan Province. As a combination of an animal sculpture and a ware, it is a perfect work of art. The body is full of relief patterns, including animal faces, a pair of dragons, tigers and phoenixes, with cloud and thunder patterns as background. The patterns integrate perfectly with the shapes. The beak-shaped nose tip and the long nose form an S-shape, which produces a sense of rhythm and flexibility. A little tiger grovels on the beak-shaped nose tip, facing the elephant's head. Two phoenixes look at each other behind the elephant's ears. Elephant-shaped bronze wares were very common during the Shang Dynasty, used during sacrificial ceremonies. The common use of Elephant *zun* is closely associated with the Shang's ecological environment. According to *Erya*, an ancient Chinese encyclopedia, there were many elephants in today's Hubei and Hunan provinces during the Shang Dynasty. They were regarded as symbols of beauty and as deities.

The other typical bronze ware is the famous *Four-Ram Square Zun*. This is a fantastic work of art with four sheep heads on four sides. It is the masterpiece among Shang bronze animal sculptures.

The various shapes and decorations of Shang bronze wares give the idea of an invisible power and a kind of devout belief in ghosts and deities. Under such spiritual power, Shang craftsmen created large numbers of ritual objects to communicate with ghosts and deities. Animal images integrated with bronze wares are, therefore, embodied with the unique characteristics of the Shang Dynasty.

Western Zhou: Simple dignity

In contrast to the gorgeous decorations and sinister shapes of the Shang period, bronze wares from the Zhou changed alongside social development. Ferocious images were forgotten as the Shang Dynasty fell into decay and simple and majestic bronze wares became dominant.

A ritual and musical system was the prominent cultural characteristic of the Zhou Dynasty. There was a defined social hierarchy, embodied by activities such as worship and the use of clothes, wares, houses, horses and chariots. The shroud of mystery shown on the decorations and shapes of Shang bronzes gradually faded.

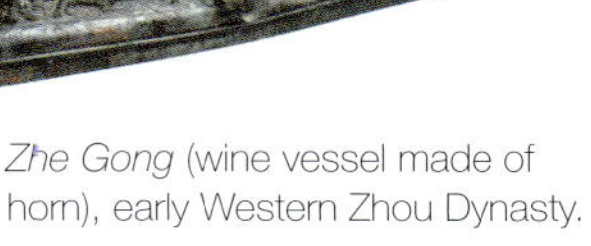

Zhe Gong (wine vessel made of horn), early Western Zhou Dynasty.

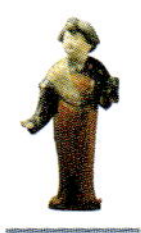

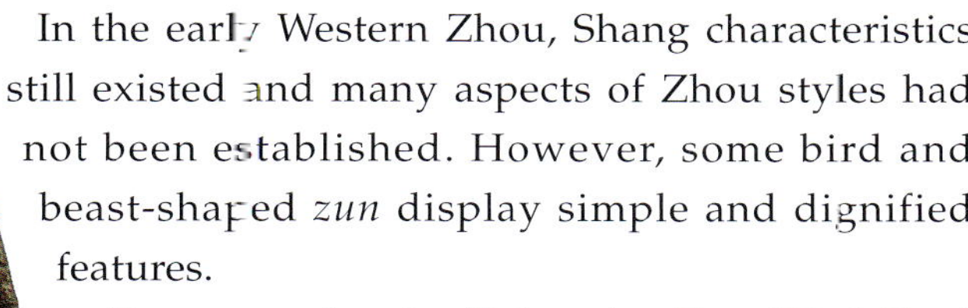

In the early Western Zhou, Shang characteristics still existed and many aspects of Zhou styles had not been established. However, some bird and beast-shaped *zun* display simple and dignified features.

For example, the *Dabaoniao Zun* (Bird *Zun*) from Xunxian County, Henan Province is a masterpiece. It is kept in the Hakutsuru Art Museum of Japan. As the styles of Zhou bronze arts were established, bird and beast-shaped *zun* changed and freed themselves from being part of wine containers. They started to develop the independent features of the sculptural arts.

Animal sculptures from the Western Zhou are a little simpler than Shang works of the same kind in decoration and shape. They have a friendly feeling and are less solemn.

Dabaoniao Zun (Bird *Zun*), early Western Zhou Dynasty.

There were also changes in details, such as the sculptural techniques used for eyes. During the Shang Dynasty, the eyes of sculptures were mostly made by a very stylized technique, known as "eye patterns."

The Western Zhou's bronze sculptures, on the other hand, began to show more vivid, lifelike features of various animals.

Western Zhou bronze sculptures do not follow complicated patterns. Their relief patterns present a new style. Some Shang patterns—including sharp and *kui* patterns—are replaced by round and gentle patterns in the Zhou, including a distinctive curled pattern that simplified earlier animal patterns.

Duck-shaped *zun*, early Western Zhou Dynasty.

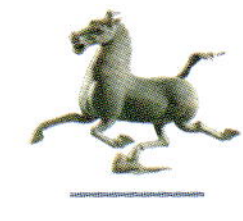

According to Master Lu's *Spring and Autumn Annals*, Zhou *Ding* had these long curled patterns. This means that this style of patterns this is present in Zhou bronze wares.

Zhou patterns do not follow the Shang style of straight lines but adopt S-shaped curves. Zhou curled patterns integrate both round and square forms. Moreover, the relief decoration patterns of Zhou bronze wares have a sense of rhythm, while quadratic sequence patterns show a sense of order closely connected with the Zhou ritual system.

In terms of the growth of Chinese sculpture, the Western Zhou Dynasty was an important turning point.

The Spring and Autumn Period and the Warring States Period: Slim and Graceful Luxury

Various ideological and cultural trends as well as artistic forms thrived during the Eastern Zhou Dynasty. Though sculptural arts had not freed themselves from crafts and architecture, the utilization of sculptural expressions became mature. The Spring and Autumn Period is regarded as a peak in the history of Chinese sculpture.

Various materials were widely used during this period, including bronze, gold, silver, lead, pottery, jade, stone, and teeth and bones from animals. The comprehensive utilization of multiple materials also began during this period. Coloring became popular. Sculptural techniques developed. Some techniques, such

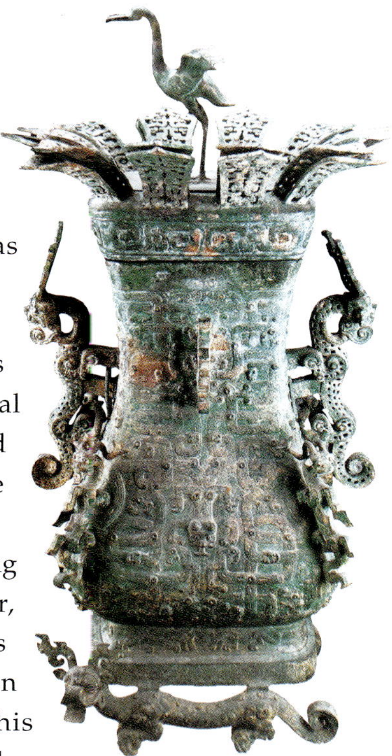

A square-shaped pot with lotus and crane designs, Spring and Autumn or the Warring States Period.

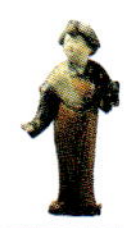

as lost-wax casting and gold and silver inlaying, push bronze sculptures into a new stage of luxurious style. The style presents the aesthetic orientation of the Spring and Autumn Period and the Warring States Period and is full of an easy and vigorous feeling.

The Eastern Zhou's animal sculptures display a high level of artistic merit and bear the signs of the times. A representative masterpiece is a square-shaped pot with lotus and crane designs from Xinzheng, Henan Province. The 122cm-high pot has dragon-shaped handles and beast-shaped feet with a double layer of lotuses on the cover. The lotus petals splay out to support a vivid immortal crane about to take flight in the center. This pot produces an agile feeling and the style has a lot to do with freedom from the ritual system.

Another typical masterpiece is the double-wing bronze divine beast inlaid with gold

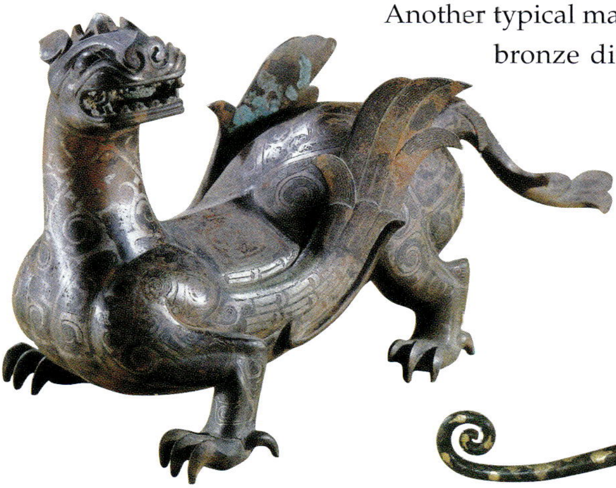

Gold- and silver-inlaid winged sacred beast, Spring and Autumn and the Warring States periods.

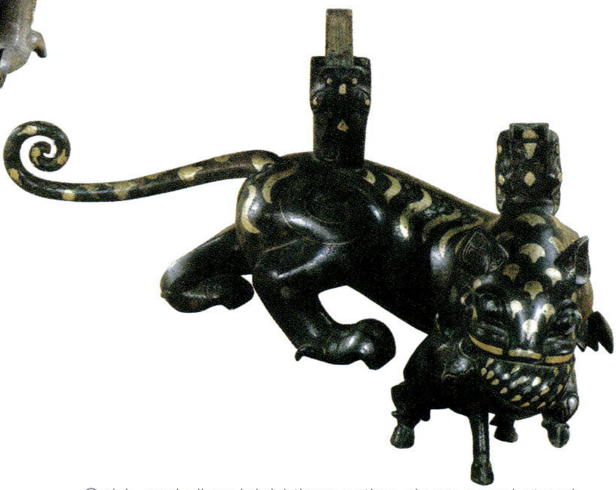

Gold- and silver-inlaid tiger-eating-deer vessel stand, Spring and Autumn and the Warring States periods.

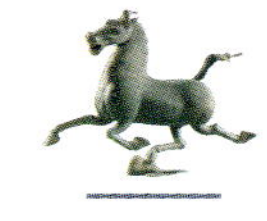

and silver unearthed from the Tomb of the King of Zhongshan Kingdom. The 40cm high sculpture integrates features of various animals—the noble quality of the dragon, the grace and power of the tiger and leopard. The divine beast is so vigorous that it seems to fly to the clouds. The sculpture is full of a sense of rhythm and vitality. It integrates motion and quietness, a traditional Chinese technique. Another similar masterpiece is the gold and silver inlaid pedestal designed with tiger-devouring-deer pattern. It is vivid and gorgeous and produces a feeling of unrest and strength, which is a symbol of the social unrest that marked the times. The gold and silver inlaying makes these sculptures more luxurious and imaginative.

An important masterpiece of the late Warring States period is the gold and silver inlaid bronze rhinoceros *zun* with cloud patterns from Xingping County, Shaanxi Province. It represents a new high in animal-shaped bronze wares of the Warring States period and displays the unique practical style of the Qin people.

The cultures of the Shang and Zhou dynasties underline the differences between different regions and their interactions. The cultures also present the heritage of different periods. Sculptures of this period mark the beginning of the history of Chinese sculpture. As it matured, Chinese sculpture established its ethnic characteristics and exerted important influence on the sculptural concepts and techniques that emerged later.

The Mysterious Culture of the Ancient Shu

Bronze Sculpture from Guanghan Sanxingdui

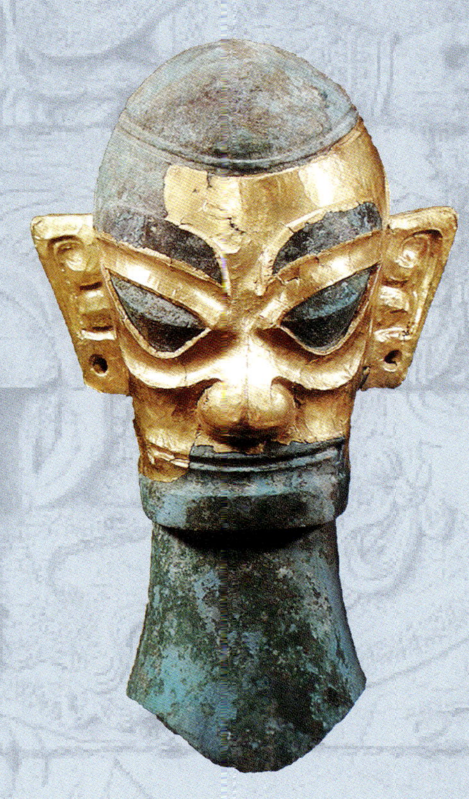

The culture of the ancient Shu, a unique civilization, grew alongside the cultures of the Central Plains during the Shang and Zhou dynasties. Large numbers of relics have been unearthed from Guanghan Sanxingdui. The bronze figures and masks are most distinctive. The styles are different from those of the Central Plains and have their own characteristics, which display the regional differences of Chinese civilization.

Sanxingdui culture

Sichuan Province was called Shu in ancient times. In the pre-Qin period, this land was home to several local tribes. They established the Kingdom of Shu but also the mysterious culture of the ancient Shu. According to the legends, several powerful tribes established a dominating position and an early kingdom.

The character "蜀" (*shu*) first surfaces in inscriptions on bones or tortoise shells from the Shang Dynasty. The history of this kingdom still remains a puzzle but the discovery of the Sanxingdui Ruins confirmed the existence of the civilization of the ancient Shu Kingdom.

The Chinese character for Sanxingdui, which means "three-star mounds," is composed of three clay piles shaped like stars. According to the *Hanzhou Annals: Mountain Annals of Jiaqing Reign of the Qing Dynasty*, there is a land of mystery in the southwest where three star-shaped clay piles shine with the moonlight. As early as the Qing Dynasty, the annals describe Sanxingdui's landform.

Actually, the three clay piles are the walls of the Shu capital, built during the Xia and Shang dynasties (2070–1046 BC). After long weathering, the old walls became clay piles.

This mysterious culture lasted for more than 2,000 years, from the late Neolithic Age to the late Shang and early Zhou dynasties. The ruins cover an area of around 1,200 hectares and are one

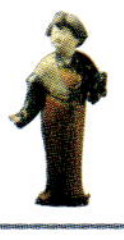

of the most important and largest cultural relics in Sichuan Province. Large numbers of pottery, jade, bronze and gold wares have been unearthed there. They have distinctive characteristics from the local culture. In contrast to the bronze cultures of the Central Plains, the objects are unlike any made in any other period of Chinese civilization. The ruins form a unique cultural system, called Sanxingdui culture.

The most important archaeological discoveries of the Sanxingdui culture were unearthed from the famous No.1 and 2 pits in the Sanxingdui Ruins. Most objects were burnt, scorched, cracked, melted or destroyed before the burial customs. Some bronze heads and masks had red mouths and dark eyes when they were found. The use of color paint was popular among many ancient civilizations, such as the ancient Greeks, who used colored paint that faded over time.

Besides some bronze, jade and pottery wares common to the Central Plains, most objects from the two pits had not been seen before, including groups of bronze figures and masks, and gold scepters and masks. The unearthed objects were not only vast in quantity but also of varying types with complicated and mysterious features. The objects and sculptures, which are unique in shape and superior in technique, obviously belong to the upper class of the ancient Shu. The ancient Shu had developed bronze-casting techniques, along with a unique aesthetic consciousness and religious beliefs.

Standing bronze figure with multiple identities

In contrast to bronze sculptures from other regions, the bronze figures from Sanxingdui have more of the features of stand alone sculptures, especially the bronze figure standing on a pedestal, which is similar to memorial sculptures of modern and contemporary times and suggests strong religious meaning. Bronze figures from Sanxingdui also present a unique spirituality in their stylized features, besides the unique majestic feeling of the Shang and Zhou's bronze sculpture. The facial casting techniques, in particular, produce a mysterious feeling and stimulate the imagination. There is still an unexplained gap between the cultural characteristics of this mysterious culture and the bronze-age culture of the Central Plains. Some have even suggested that these civilizations are of extraterrestrial origin. However, archaeological excavations prove that the Sanxingdui culture was indeed established by the Shu people.

Among the bronze sculptures from Sanxingdui, the tallest and best-preserved standing bronze figure is 260.8cm high. It consists of a 180cm figure and an 80.8cm base. It was cast in separate components with a hollow body. It is wearing a flower-shaped high crown and a gorgeous short-sleeved robe engraved with dragons, birds and exotic animal patterns. It has extraordinary large ring-shaped hands, arms in embracing gesture in front of its chest, and its bare feet are wearing anklets. Under the feet is a high base decorated with various patterns. The

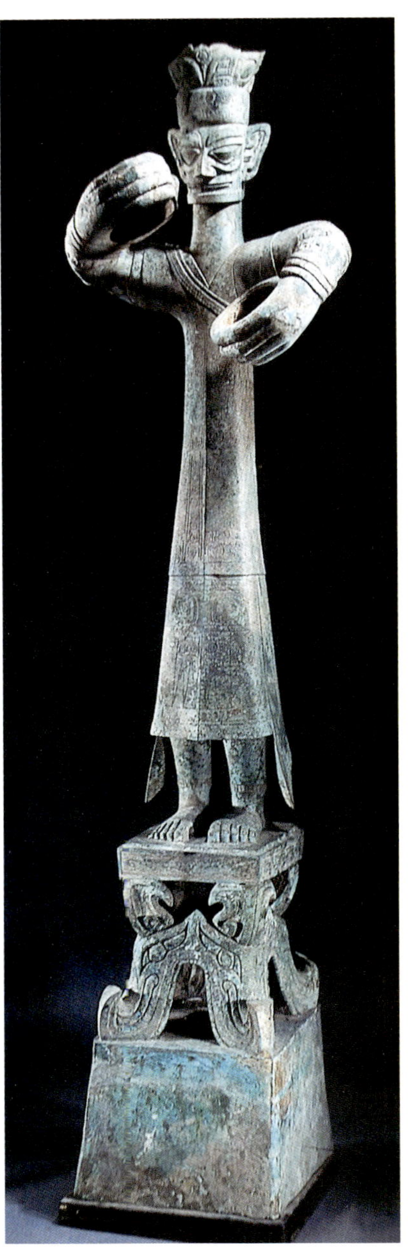

Standing bronze figure, late Shang Dynasty.

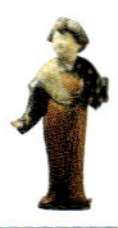

figure looks very solemn. The casting technique is exquisite. Academics regard this monumental standing figure as the image of a king from Shu, who was also a high priest. In ancient Shu, the king held the leading political and religious position. The kingdom was similar to a theocracy. So, this figure presents both a priest presiding over a worship ceremony and a representative of deities accepting worship. The figure once held something in its ring-shaped hand which has sadly been lost.

Unexplained bronze heads

Besides the standing bronze figure, most of the unearthed bronze sculptures from Sanxingdui are independent bronze heads, some of which have gold foil masks. Because these bronze heads look strange, some people have claimed that they are alien objects.

For example, a 45.8cm bronze head with round vertex and gold foil mask was unearthed from the No.2 pit. In view of the facial contour, a bronze mask covered its face and head. It is clear that a gold foil mask was attached to the bronze mask afterwards. The gold foil mast is very thin and has been damaged. A hairpin with damaged ends decorates the back of the head.

Another bronze head with gold mask from the same pit is a little different. It has a flat vertex with hair plaited at the back and put up with a broad hair tie at the top. It presents the profound cultural features of the local people and the way local people dressed.

A bronze head with gold mask, late Shang Dynasty.

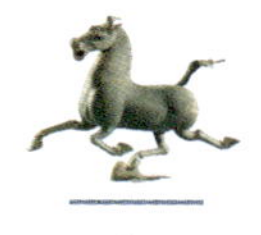

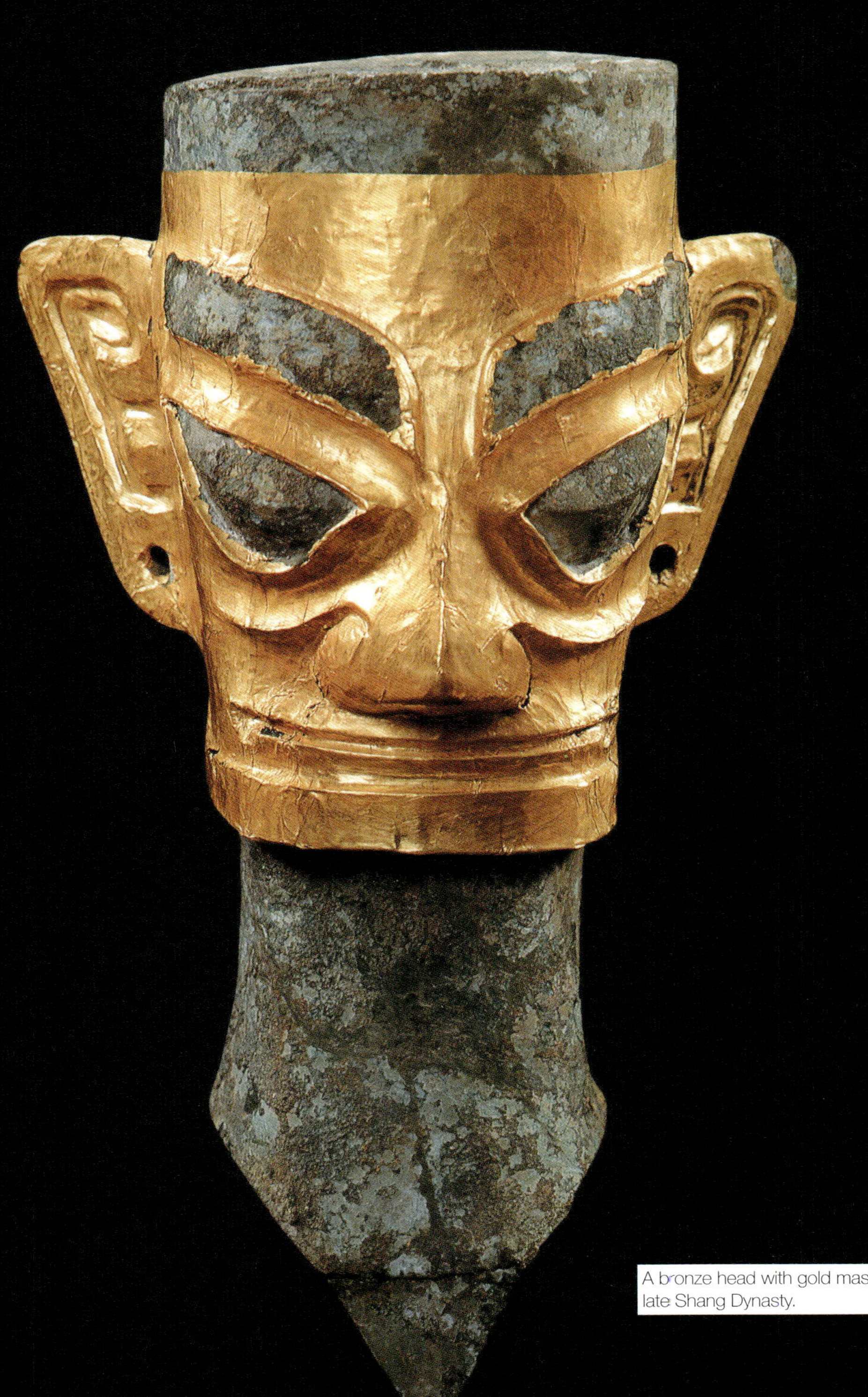

A bronze head with gold mask, late Shang Dynasty.

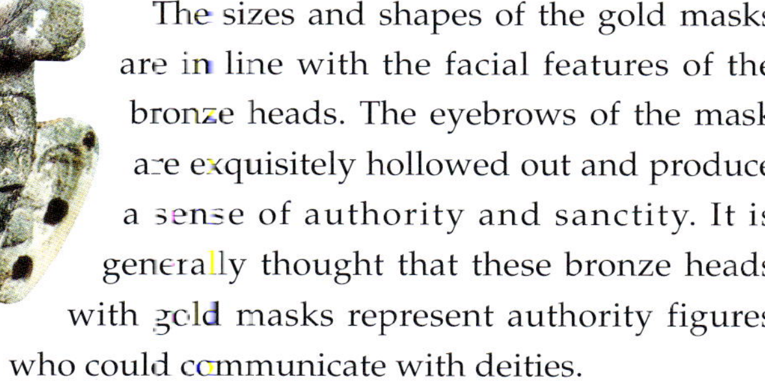

A bronze human head, late Shang Dynasty.

The sizes and shapes of the gold masks are in line with the facial features of the bronze heads. The eyebrows of the mask are exquisitely hollowed out and produce a sense of authority and sanctity. It is generally thought that these bronze heads with gold masks represent authority figures who could communicate with deities.

Another two bronze heads unearthed from the No.2 pit are also very distinctive but without the gold masks. One hatchet-faced bronze head is 13.6cm in height with knife-shaped eyebrows, big eyes, typical snub nose, wide mouth and big ears. The Shu people highlight such facial features with exaggeration and stylized features. On top, the head has a plait-and-band-shaped decoration, which may be plaited hair or a decoration to secure a crown, which is also similar to the dressing style of some areas in today's Sichuan. The bronze head has a clear shape and an honest and sincere face full of local characteristics.

The other 51.6cm-high bronze head wears a hair stick without a gold mask. It is an integral piece made by the whole casting technique. It has a round vertex and looks like it is wearing a helmet. There are butterfly-shaped hair ornaments at the back of head. Its hair is put up with a broad band in the middle. It also shares similar facial features, including a snub nose, wide mouth and straight ears. It has apparent black painting on eyebrows and eye sockets and red painting on the earholes and nostrils and between the lips.

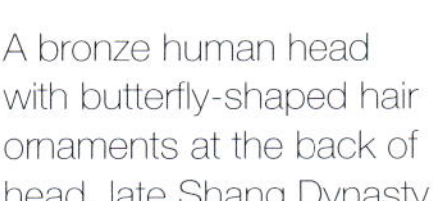

A bronze human head with butterfly-shaped hair ornaments at the back of head, late Shang Dynasty.

A unique bronze head, widely regarded as a female image, was unearthed from the No.1 pit of Sanxingdui. The top of the head is damaged and there could have been hair ornaments or a crown on top. The hairline at the back of head is clear. It also has vertical eyes and snub nose, but its ears are a little smaller than those of other sculptures. Its lips are sealed. Its mouth is more natural and narrow than others. There is a smile on its face. Its facial features are full of fluency with a lively face and a wide jaw. It seems to reflect mild and quiet temperament.

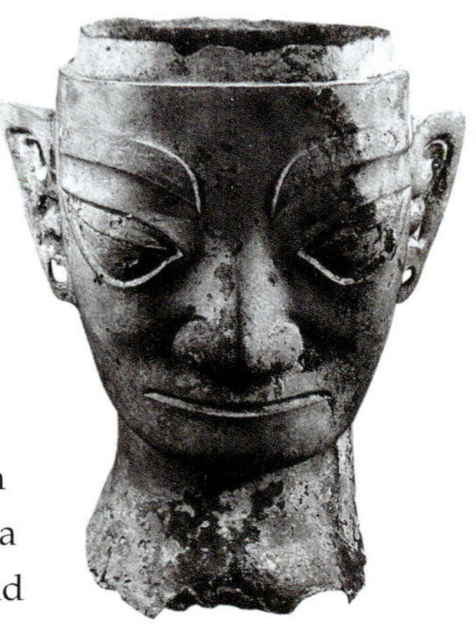

A bronze female head, late Shang Dynasty.

Large bronze masks with vertical eyes and straight ears

Besides the standing bronze figure and bronze heads, some large bronze masks from Sanxingdui are also very striking. The most distinctive and imposing is the bronze mask with vertical eyes and straight ears. This mask has bulging eyes and monstrously protruding eyeballs like two cylinders. A total of three bronze masks with vertical eyes were unearthed from the No.2 pit of Sanxingdui and reflect two styles, A and B. They have similar shapes but two major differences.

The first is the forehead. Mask A has a fine frontlet, several dozen centimeters in height. Mask B has a square hole in the center of forehead (used to install subsidiary ornaments that no longer exist).

Second is the size and shape of the ears. The B mask has a pair of fully expanded ears with a peach tip-shaped top. The ears of B produce a feeling of flying. Although the ears of the A mask are similar to those of B, they are less exaggerated and in a straight and flat shape.

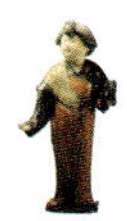

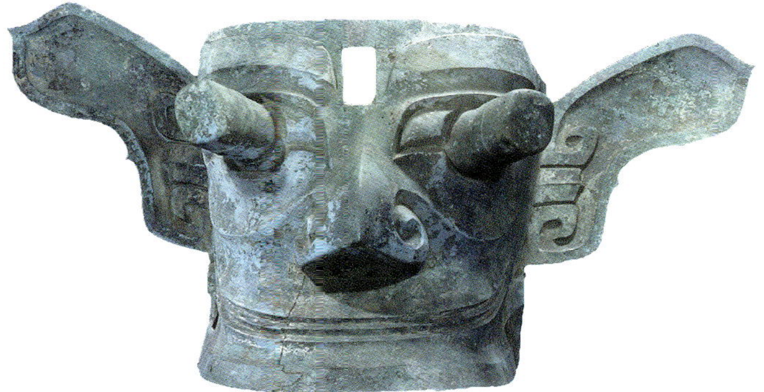

The bronze mask with exaggerated eyes, late Shang Dynasty.

The representative B mask is a bronze vertical mask, whose eyes and ears are extremely exaggerated. It is called "clairvoyant" and "clairaudient." According to ancient Chinese legends, there are two deities. One possesses the power of clairvoyance. The other possesses the power of clairaudience. The exaggerated look of the mask is suggestive of these two deities. However, there are no records to prove that these masks are their embodiment. This huge bronze mask is 138cm wide and 66cm high. Its brow tips rise upward. Its eyes are crossed and the eyeballs are extremely exaggerated, bulging forward to 16cm. The upper parts of its square-shaped ears expand outward like peaches. Its nose is short and the mouth large and wide. The mouth corners are lifted upward, as if smiling. There is a square hole in the forehead, for a fine frontlet. It would be more exquisite and majestic if were complete, but it still delivers a charming surrealism.

Why were objects with mysterious looks made by the ancient Shu? They were likely connected with images of deities and ancestors. It is said that the ancestors of the Shu people were the Can Cong, whose facial features are similar to the mask. According to ancient Chinese legend, there is a deity called Zhu Long, who has a pair of "straight eyeballs" like the bulging eyes on the mask. Therefore, the mask may be closely associated with the ancestor and deity worship of the Shu people.

Another distinctive mask with a frontlet is 82.5cm high and has similar, extremely exaggerated eyeballs, which bulge forward to 10cm. On its forehead, a 70cm high *kui*-shaped frontlet is casted. This *kui*-shaped pattern is different from those of the Central Plains and of the Shu style. This bronze mask has black painting on the eyes and eyebrows and red painting on lips. It is mysterious in shape and eerie and beautiful in style. Its eyes are in line with the recorded features of the eyes of Can Cong. The *kui*-shaped frontlet suggests a close connection with Zhu Long, a legendary deity with straight eyeballs, the head of human and the body of dragon.

The bronze figures from Sanxingdui give us a majestically stylized feeling and an unusual sense of dimension. The mysterious Shu culture has faded away, but we can still feel the cultural impact of these silent and stately bronze sculptures.

Kui

Kui is an animal similar to a dragon in ancient Chinese fables. It differs from the dragon as it is said to have only one foot. Since ancient artists used to use two feet for four and one foot for two when portraying the sides of animals, the saying that "*Kui* has one foot" came into existence. This is one of the key patterns on bronze ware from the Shang and Zhou dynasties.

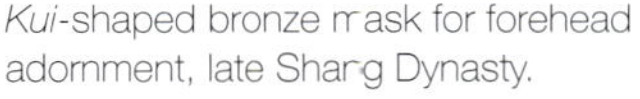

Kui-shaped bronze mask for forehead adornment, late Shang Dynasty.

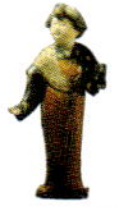

Emperor Qin Shihuang's Underground Army

The Terracotta Warriors and Horses and Bronze Chariots from the Qin Dynasty

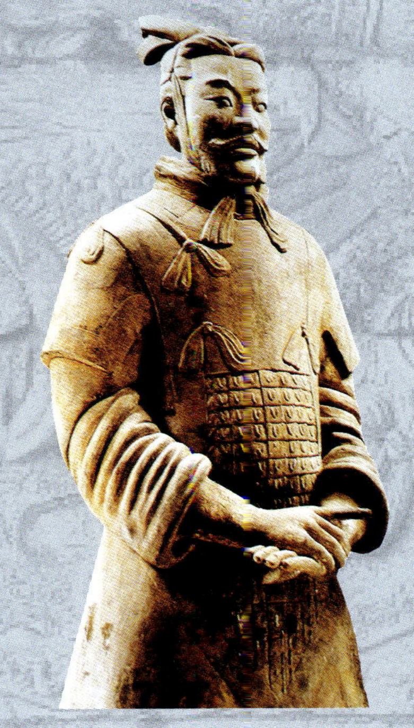

During the Qin and Han dynasties (221 BC–AD 220), with the establishment and consolidation of a unified dynasty, emperors ordered the construction of an "underground army:" the terracotta warriors and horses. The figures made during the reign of Emperor Shihuang of the Qin Dynasty (the first Qin Dynasty emperor) are the best. The charm of these figures can be seen on each sculpture - realistic, precise, vivid, powerful and awesome.

Qin Shi Huang, the first emperor of a unified China left many important cultural relics from his reign of less than fifteen years. The terracotta warriors and horses are a message of the power of the Qin and the ambition of Emperor Shihuang to his descendants.

What are tomb figures?

When Emperor Shihuang unified the other six states in 221 BC, the tomb figures were created. No large-scale, realistic tomb figures like Qin terracotta figures had been seen before. The tomb figures from the Shang, the Spring and Autumn Period and the Warring States Period were small and unrealistic. They are not as vivid or impressive as the Qin terracotta figures.

How did tomb figures emerge?

During the Shang and Zhou dynasties, people were buried alive in tombs with the deceased as sacrifices. Slaves were buried with their owners, as clearly demonstrated by archeological digs of Shang Dynasty institutions. As society evolved, this practice was gradually replaced by burying clay

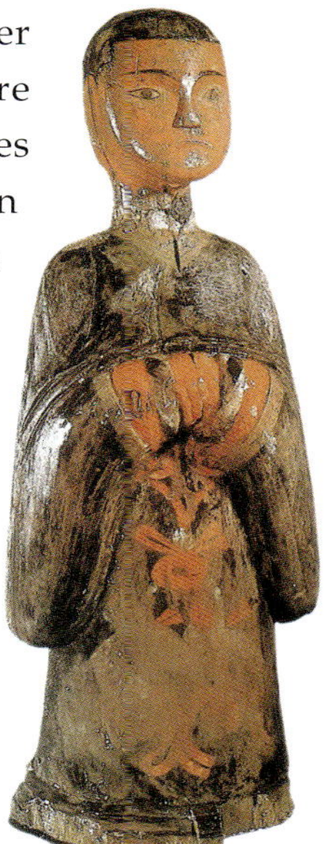

Painted wooden figurine, Spring and Autumn and the Warring States periods.

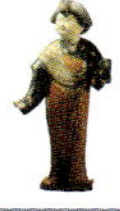

sculptures, woodcarvings or bronze figures. Burying tomb figures became popular during the Qin Dynasty and reached a peak with the terracotta figures.

Excavation of the Qin Terracotta warriors and horses

There are no detailed records of when the Qin terracotta warriors and horses were built by Emperor Shihuang. Perhaps he hoped not to be disturbed by later generations. These mighty

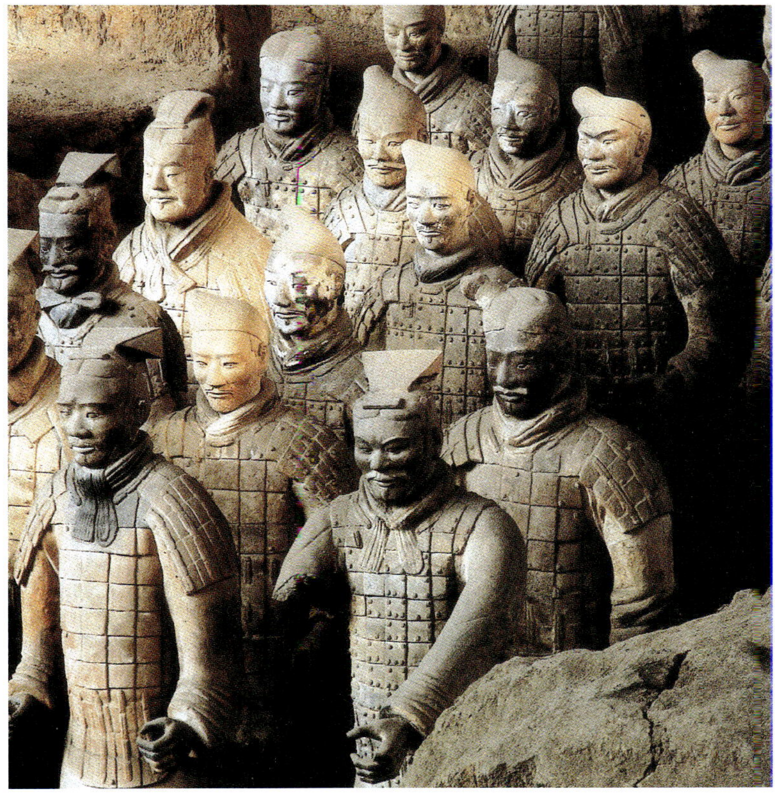

Terracotta warriors, Qin Dynasty.

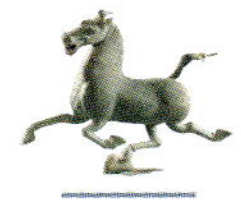

warriors and horses were discovered more than 2,000 years later by chance. A group of peasants uncovered some pottery while digging for a well nearby in 1974. A few years later, the Museum of Qin Terracotta Warriors and Horses was built. It opened in 1979.

The discovery of the Qin terracotta warriors and horses stirred the world. The statues were recognized as a cultural miracle from ancient times and one of the most important discoveries of the modern era.

The terracotta warriors and horses were found about 1.5km east of Emperor Qin Shihuang's Mausoleum in Lintong County, Shaanxi Province. It is a sight that should not be missed by any visitor to China.

The No.1, 2 and 3 pits were discovered first. The No.1 pit is the largest, with a total area of 14,260 square meters. About 6,000 life sized pottery figures are buried in this pit. It is truly incredible that so many large sized and pottery figures were made. The Qin Terracotta warriors and horses are broad in scale and have an impressive appearance. They are finely and carefully portrayed, showing the superb skills of Qin craftsmen and their ability to master the relationship between the whole and details.

Of the figures, nearly 1,000 lifesize terracotta warriors arranged in battle formations were excavated five meters below the earth. They are powerful and awesome. Besides the warriors, some ceramic horses were found, also identical to authentic horses in size. There are also chariots with four horses.

Some warriors wear coats of armor; some are dressed in mail with bronze weapons in their hands. These weapons are real objects. The army was strictly arranged in a battle formation. Dozens of horses raise their heads, neighing and galloping forward. The whole army is ready. The mighty army represents the brutal military conquest involved in the unification of China.

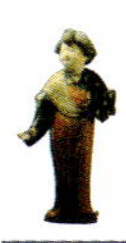

Shape of the Qin Terracotta Warriors and Horses

The shape of Qin terracotta figures is based on actual life. The clothing and appearance of each figure is unique. There are several hairstyles, gestures and facial expressions. People can judge whether they are officials or soldiers from their clothes, expressions and gestures. In general, all the Qin terracotta figures show expressions of dignity and elegance with vivid personality and intense features.

The Terracotta Warriors and Horses are sculpted and painted. The color on the faces and clothes could be seen clearly when they were unearthed. The sculptural techniques used are flexible, producing figures that are authentic, unique and expressive. On account of this, the Qin Terracotta Warriors and Horses occupy an important position in the history of Chinese sculpture.

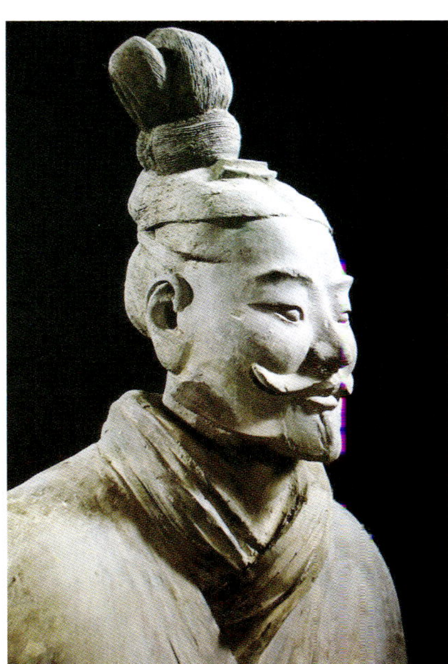

Head of warrior in battle robe, Qin Dynasty

Of more than 1,000 unearthed figures, no two are identical. Most notable are the differences between expressions and facial forms. The military officers are serious and older with some wrinkles on their foreheads, and the warriors' expressions are individualized, showing distinct characteristics of different regions. The facial features of many Qin

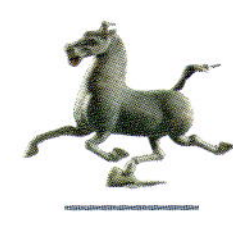

warriors are thought to be close to those of the people of Shaanxi Province.

All the terracotta warriors have martial bearings, suggesting a heroic spirit and representing the might of Qin Shihuang's ambition of "conquering six states and unifying China."

The terracotta figures can be divided into two categories depending on their status: warriors and military officers. The military officers also have low, medium and high grades. The warriors do not wear caps but the military officers are coroneted. The crowns of common officers are different from those of the generals. Even the armors are different. The soldiers include foot soldiers, cavalry, and chariot soldiers. The foot soldiers do not wear armor but instead wear leg wrappings, which are convenient for running. The warriors who drive the chariots have shields. These terracotta figures originally held arrows or long weapons, but when unearthed most of the weapons were not in their hands but scattered in the pits. The bronze weapons unearthed from the pits include swords, spears, lances, curved knives and a large numbers of crossbows and arrows. These alloy weapons are still very sharp thanks to a chromizing treatment, even after being buried more than 2,000 years. This indicates that metallurgy technology was relatively sophisticated at that time.

Making these figures so precisely and so realistically was not easy. The challenges are determined by the nature of the clay, which requires remarkable skills and rich experience. Pottery figures collapse easily and faults in the molding and firing show up quickly. Qin Dynasty craftsmen used molding, piling, kneading, pasting, carving, painting and other techniques to make the figures perfect in terms of body, spirit, color and quality. Craftsmen could have used mud to shape the legs of warriors, and then formed the body using armor and clothes as the mold. Heads must have been shaped individually

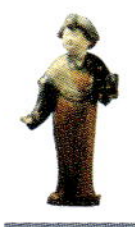

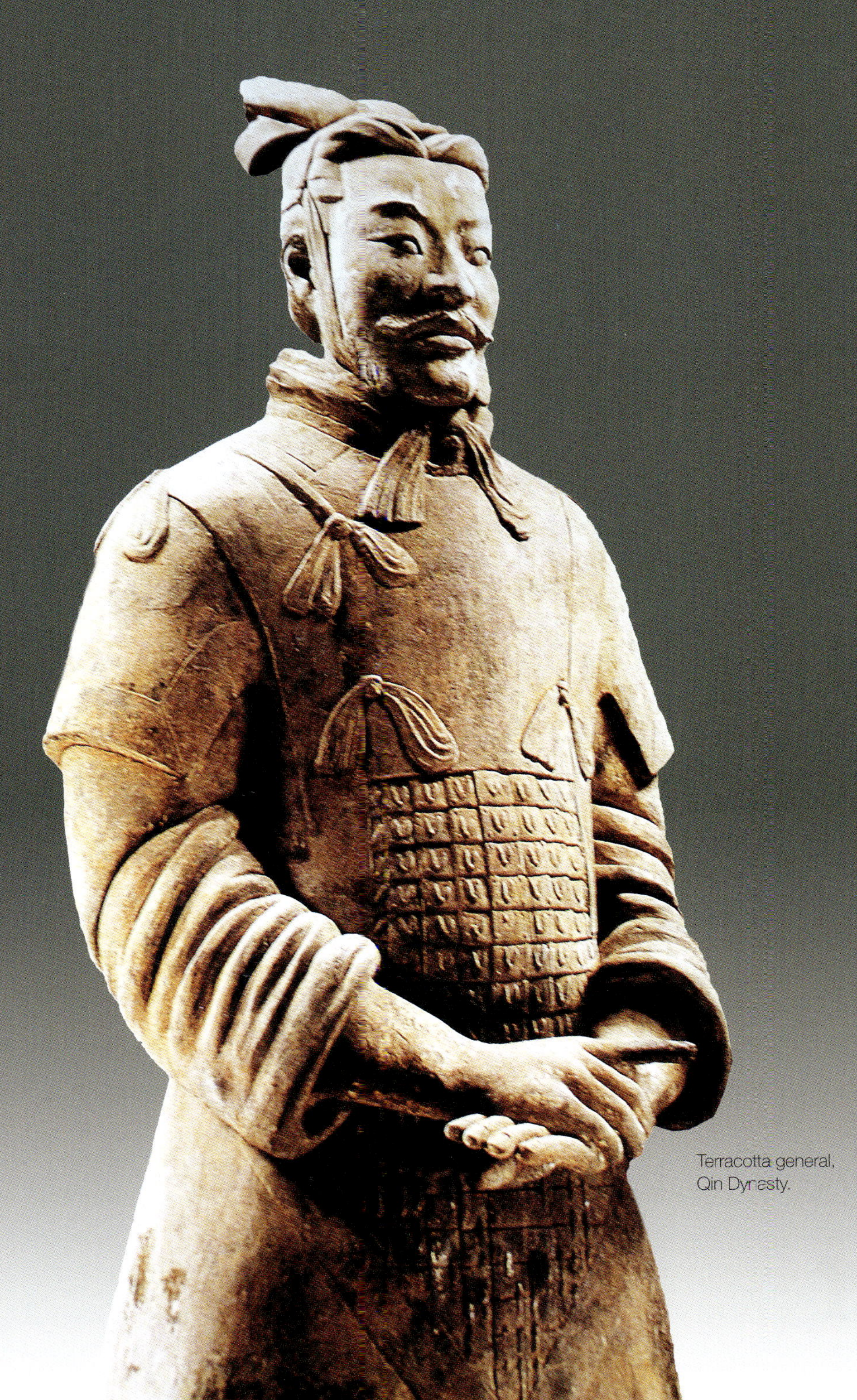

Terracotta general,
Qin Dynasty.

to make each figure quite different from the others. All these factors require sophisticated levels of firing technology. The thickness of the pottery shard should be balanced and the temperature and level of attainment suitable.

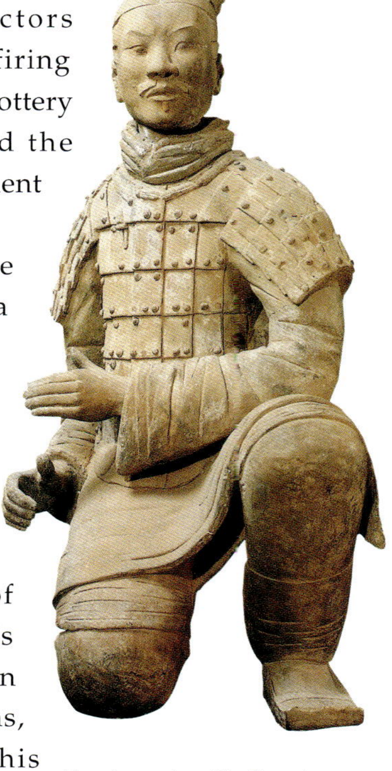
Kneeling archer, Qin Dynasty.

Two figures in particular are unforgettable. One is the Terracotta General. Another is the Kneeling Terracotta Soldier. The general is 1.96m tall. He is standing lofty and firm and lost in thought. He shows an expression of unyielding power. He suggests the simple, martial character of Qin warriors. The success of this terracotta figure lies not only in exquisite design and proportions, but also in the conveyance of his character. The general's appearance is serious and calm, more confident than the warriors with ferocious expressions. The general's wisdom and stateliness is reflected in the pottery figure.

Fight and Love with a Terracotta Warrior is a 1989 film about forbidden love between a court lady and a soldier during the Qin Dynasty. The soldier was reborn 2,000 years later after the reincarnation of the girl, who remembers nothing, enters the grave of Emperor Qin to find a living ancient warrior. The Qin terracotta warriors have inspired many romantic stories.

The Kneeling Terracotta Soldiers are a perfect example of the Qin craftsmen's mastery of the structure of the human body.

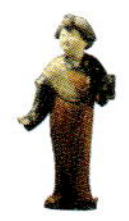

These soldiers always have their left legs bent and right legs touching the ground. Their eyes are to the front and two hands hold the crossbow. They look poised and calm.

Terracotta horses and bronze chariots

The terracotta horses also used real horses as models. The horses are about 2m long, 1.3m tall at the shoulder and 1.5m tall at the head. Their two eyes look to the front with their long mouths open slightly and four legs jumping out, ready to go out to battle. Some fore legs seem like pillars, some hind legs look like bows and the ankles are slim, showing the characteristics of

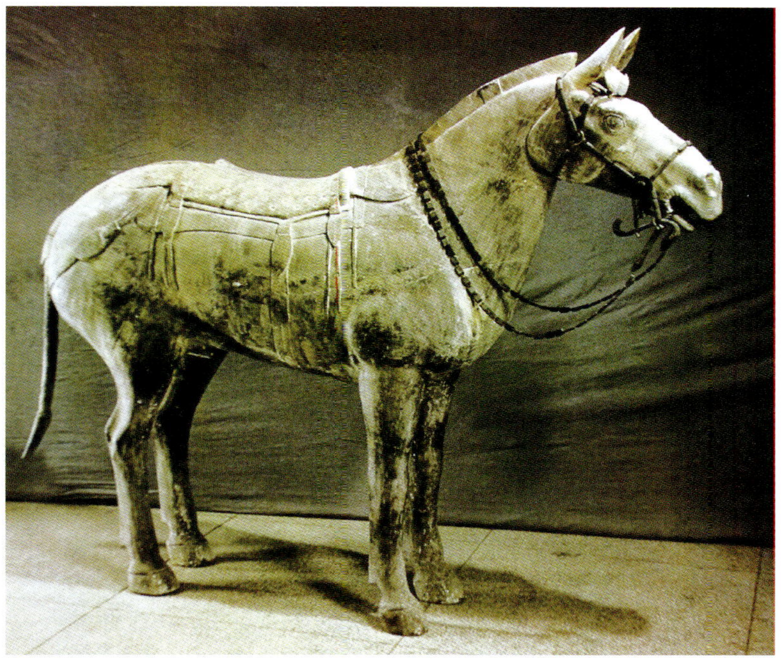

Terracotta horses, Qin Dynasty.

racehorses. They are the biggest terracotta horses unearthed in China to this day.

The curves of the body are harmonious between hard and soft and the muscle is full of strength. Although the terracotta horses are static, they seem very vigorous. Even the teeth were designed very carefully. If a horse has six teeth, it indicates that the horse is young. These vivid terracotta horses remind people that the horses that accompanied Emperor Shihuang were used in battle. They have fair-sounding names, such as *Zhuifeng* (Drive the Wind), *Zhutu* (Chase the Rabbit), *Nieying* (Chase the Shadow). Each horse displays overwhelming strength.

Another important archeological discovery of Qin Dynasty sculpture is the bronze chariots and horses. After the Qin Terracotta Warriors and Horses were unearthed, two sets of large painted bronze chariots and horses were unearthed in 1980 near the tomb of the first emperor of the Dynasty. Each set has four horses and one driver. The size of the horses and chariot is about one third of the real size.

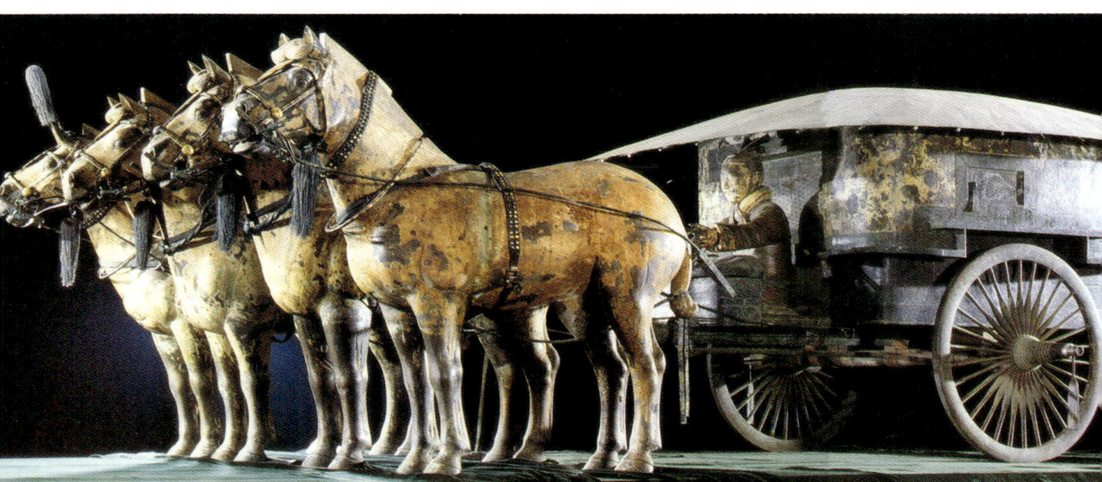

Bronze chariots and horses, Qin Dynasty.

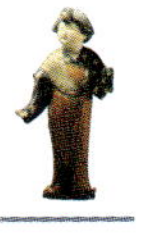

These chariots were gorgeously adorned and no detail was overlooked. The coloring is well preserved. The carving technique is even better than that used on the pottery figures. The structure is complicated and accurate, and truly represents the characteristics of the Qin Dynasty.

Chinese realism

Manner Portrayal
In China, the criterion of "manner portrayal" was established in the Wei, Jin and the Northern and Southern dynasties. At that time, there was a famous painter named Gu Kaizhi who not only made great achievements in painting but established an important theory related to painting. He held that the most important aspect in terms of portraying a person lies in the delivery of their manner and temperament, and that this manner mainly shows itself in the portrayal of the eyes. His view exerted a profound influence over the following generation. There were no writings about the artistic criterion of "manner portrayal" in the Qin Dynasty, but we can feel the importance of "manner portrayal" in the sculpture of the Terracotta Warriors. In fact, "manner portrayal" has existed in China's artistic tradition for over 1,000 years.

The realistic characteristics of the Qin terracotta warriors represent a kind of Chinese realism: although the basic pattern is realistic, it breaks through the limitation of realism. It combines the imagination of the sculptors of the Qin Dynasty They made every effort, including "manner portrayal", to grasp the characteristic and to make suitable exaggerations. For example, the warriors' thumbs are longer to increase the sense of strength. The heads of the horses are square, the eyes are big, the noses and mouths are wide and the body is round. Therefore, the horses seem very strong.

The hairstyles of the Qin warriors are also based on the true features of the time. The armor is shaped very delicately and exactly like the true armor. Even the band connecting the armor, belt hooks, bandages and bootlaces are carefully engraved. We can imagine the true appearance of warriors in the Qin Dynasty from these clothes and ornaments.

Qin Dynasty sculpture shows realism and majesty. Unlike the terracotta figures of the Han Dynasty, they encourage a military spirit, while the Han Dynasty worshipped Confucianism. Sculpture from the Qin Dynasty inherited earlier realism and

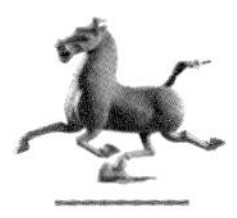

expanded it in terms of style and skills. It underlines how Chinese sculpture became mature and began to form its unique style.

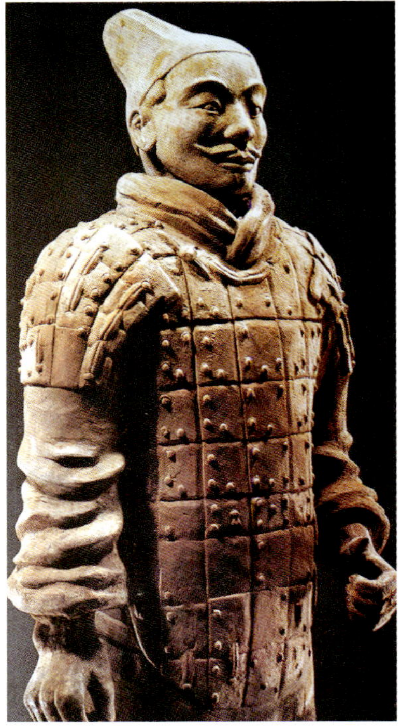

Terracotta warrior in armor, Qin Dynasty.

Magnificent Stone Carvings from the Han Dynasty

The Tomb of Huo Qubing and Carved Stone Animals from the Eastern Han Dynasty

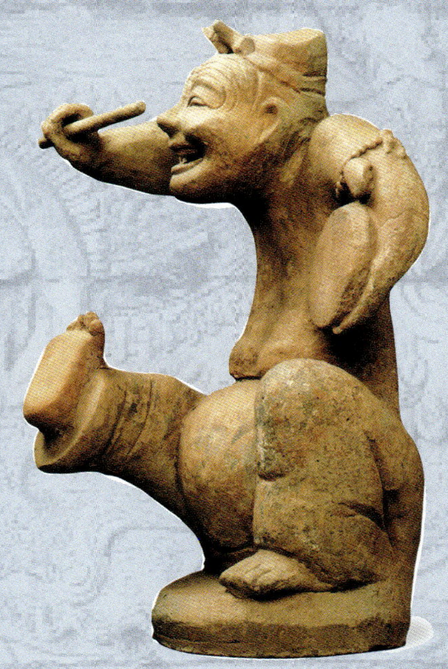

The Han Dynasty inherited a system from the Qin Dynasty. The emperors of the Western Han Dynasty adopted the custom of using terracotta warriors and horses as burial objects. But their terracotta figures are not as splendid and mighty as the Qin terracotta figures. Figures from the Han Dynasty reflect the charm of the culture of the Chu Kingdom - romantic and humorous with cultural features. The most distinct sculptures of the Han Dynasty are the well-known stone carvings from the tomb of Huo Qubing, a young general serving in the army of Emperor Wu. These stone carvings are of great importance.

The stones were carved based on their original shape using the skills of relief, line carving and circular carving. Thus the stone carvings, like nature itself, have a sense of strength. The carving skills reflect the courage of the young general and the depth of Han culture.

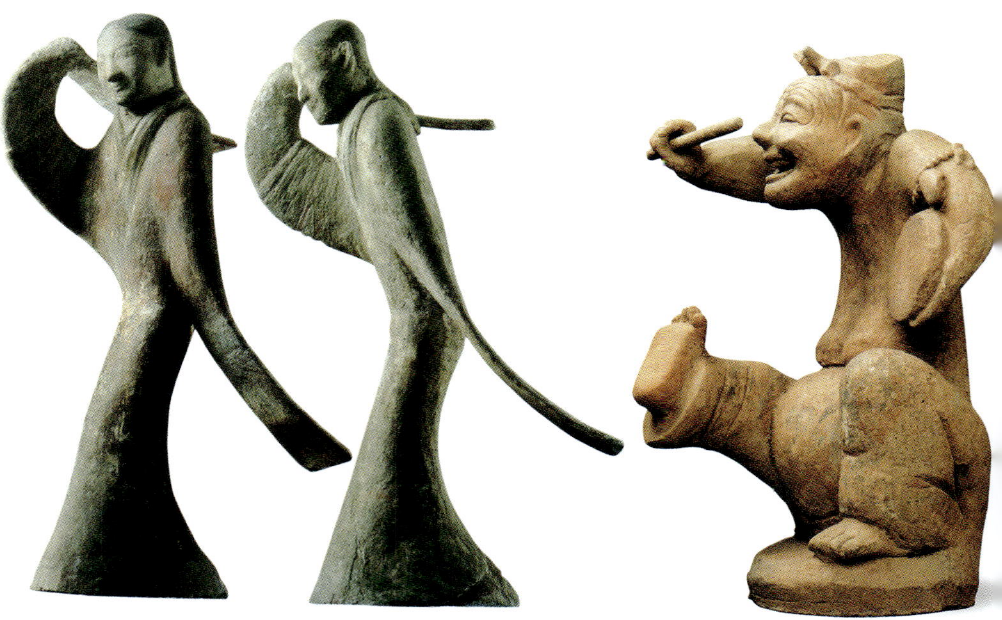

Pottery dancing-girl figurines, Western Han Dynasty.

Pottery performing figurine, Eastern Han Dynasty.

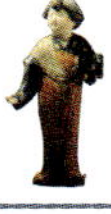

Large stone carvings

Sculptural art from the Han Dynasty achieved new heights due to developments in palace and mausoleum construction, especially in the development of large stone carvings.

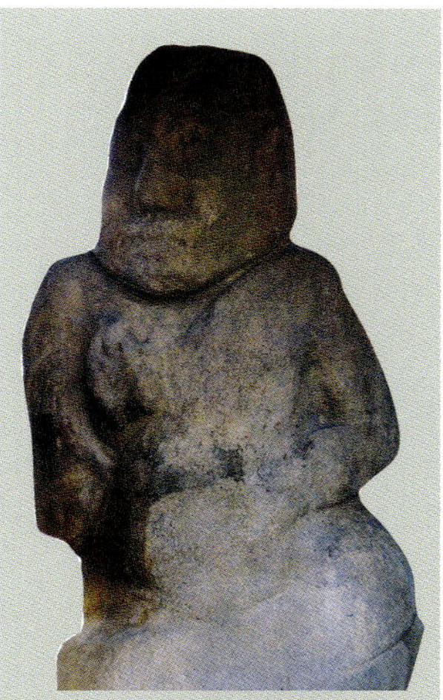

Herd Boy, Western Han Dynasty.

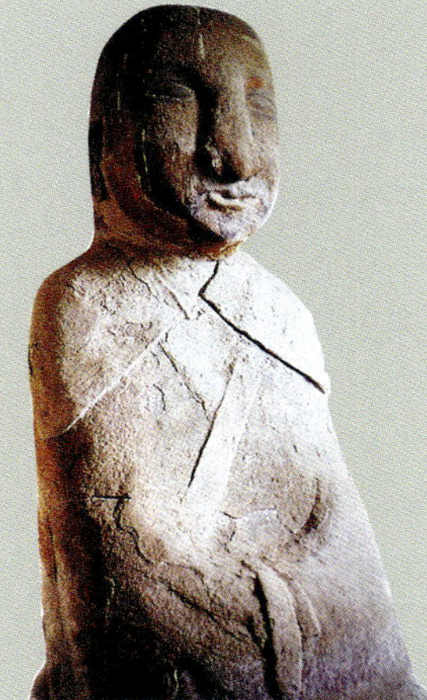

Spinning Damsel, Western Han Dynasty.

The earliest large stone carvings in China are the stone statues of the Spinning Damsel and the Herd Boy in Shaanxi Province. The statues are about three miles apart from east to west. According to the *Biography of Emperor Wudi*, the statues were made in the third year of Emperor Wudi's reign (120 BC).

The statues of the Spinning Damsel and the Herd Boy were set on the eastern and western banks of Kunming Pond, so the statues are also called Stone Carvings at Kunming Pond. The statue of the Herd Boy is 258cm tall with his right hand on the chest, left hand close to his stomach, kneeling down. The statue of the Spinning Damsel is 228cm tall with her hands in her sleeves.

This group of statues is based on the ancient Chinese legend of the Spinning Damsel and the Herd Boy. They show the classical simple style of stone carvings during the Han Dynasty. They are representative of early Chinese garden sculptures. The style of the Kunming Pond and the carved tomb of Huo Qubing show the development of sculpture during the Han Dynasty.

The Western Han Dynasty was still an early stage in traditional Chinese culture, but pottery figures from this period indicate the strong cultural features and the romanticism of Chu culture as well as the interests of people at that time.

The tomb of Huo Qubing

Huo Qubing is known for two factors: his brilliant military success during the Han Dynasty and the artistic achievement of his tomb.

Huo Qubing (140–117 BC) was an outstanding and brave general during the Western Han Dynasty. He led his troops to repulse numerous incursions by the Xiongnu and brought peace and prosperity to society. He worked as army commandant when he was eighteen years old and died at the early age of twenty-four due to plague. During this period, he repelled multiple invasions by the Xiongnu. His most famous victory took place at Qilian Mountain. The troops of Xiongnu had long occupied northern China, and their defeat not only relieved the troubles in the northwest, but also opened the *Hexi* Corridor leading to ancient *Xiyu* (western regions).

Emperor Wudi (156–87 BC) and the entire nation mourned the death of this war hero, so the emperor gave orders to hold a ceremonial funeral for Huo Qubing and built a spacious tomb for him just beside his own.

In ancient China, being buried in the imperial mausoleum was a great honor. According to historical records, more than twenty tombs were found in the mausoleum of Emperor Wudi, all of great statesmen, famous warriors, concubines and relatives of the emperor. The building of the tomb of Huo Qubing showed how much the emperor valued this young general.

On the mound of the tomb, the pile of earth symbolizes the Qilian Mountain, to commemorate Huo Qubing's outstanding achievements in that place. The stone carvings include the Horse

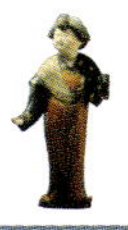

Stepping on a Xiongnu Soldier, Kneeling Horse, Galloping Horse, Yield Tiger, Lying Elephant, Stone Fish, Stone Frog, Bull, Giant Fights a Bear, Monster Bites Sheep and others. These stone carvings scattered in front of the tomb of Huo Qubing became part of the natural environment. The stone carvings represent the scene of Qilian Mountain and the fierce battle at the time, as well as the victory scene after the battle of Qilianshan.

Horse Stepping on a Xiongnu Soldier

These stone carvings are eye-catching for their artistic expression. The carvings are not very refined, but are made with crude rock and little carving. They look very powerful. The horses, carved in three different postures—stepping, lying and galloping—remind people of the valiant general and his warriors.

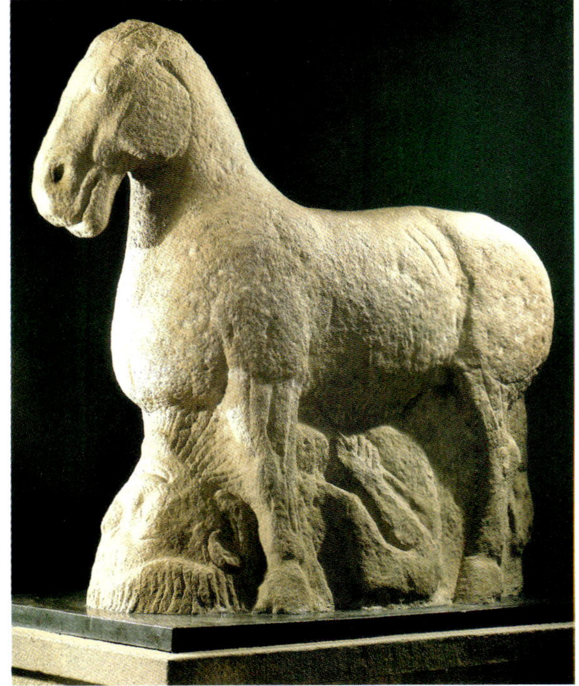

Horse Stepping on a Xiongnu Soldier, Western Han Dynasty.

One of the most excellent among the many stone carvings of domesticated and wild animals in the tomb is the Horse Stepping on a Xiongnu Soldier. The sculpture vividly displays the great power of the Western Han Dynasty and Huo Qubing's immense military contribution. The horse is brave, strong, placid and firm. The soldier under its feet, although in the panicked last moments of his life, has a fierce

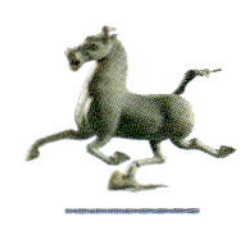

expression. Even though his failure is destined, he still holds his weapon, as if putting up a desperate last struggle.

Making a Tomb-Qilian Mountain

These stone carvings have a direct relationship with Qilian Mountain. The stones on the tomb are also arranged in the shape of Qilian Mountain, hence "making the tomb a Qilian Mountain." The Galloping Horse and Lying Horse present the rural and pastoral landscape after winning the Xiongnu. The galloping horse symbolizes the vitality of life and the lush grass. It is 145cm tall and 240cm long and is carved into a huge stone. Its hind legs are bent, the fore legs humped and the head flung back. The carvings on the fore legs and hind legs are very prominent, giving the stone horse a strong and dynamic posture. The lying horse and ox are strong but calm with a heavy, quiet air that suggests a quiet and harmonious life.

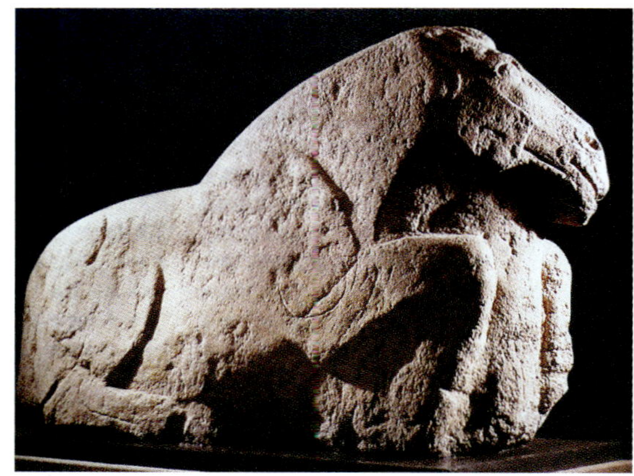

Galloping Horse, Western Han Dynasty.

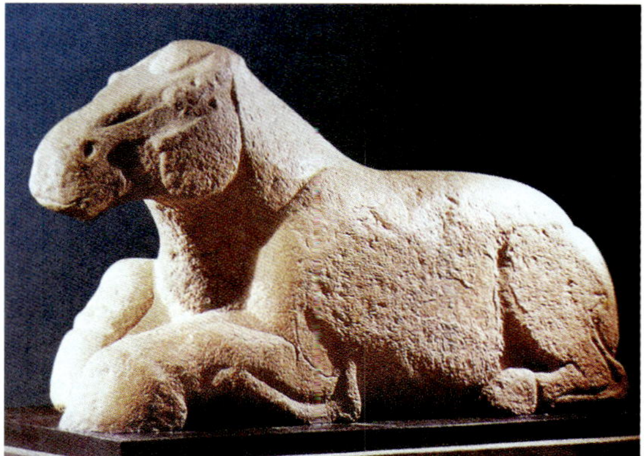

Lying Horse, Western Han Dynasty.

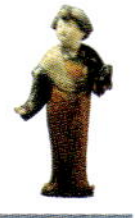

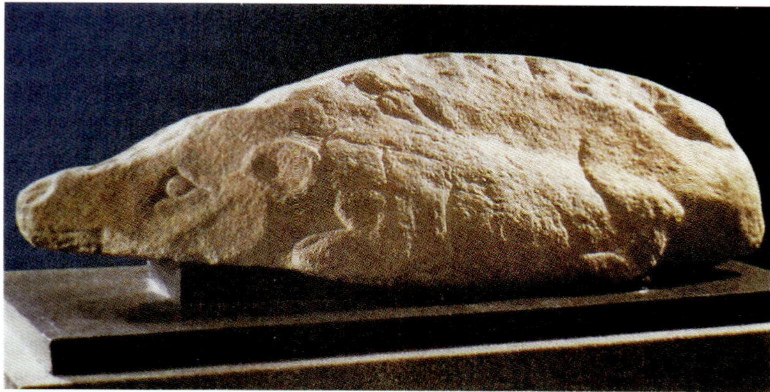

Boar Western, Han Dynasty.

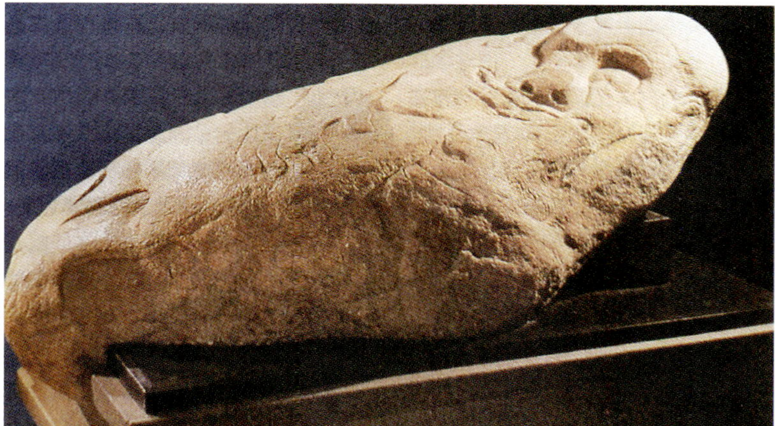

A Giant Fights a Bear, Western Han Dynasty.

There are also some stone carvings that describe battle, such as the stone carvings of Giant Fights a Bear and Monster Bites *Sheep*. They represent a life-and-death fight between people and beasts and are reminiscent of the difficulties and dangers of the battlefield. The stone carving of Giant Fights A Bear is carved in low relief on a piece of 277cm-long and 172cm-wide stone. The figure is crude and primitive but it gives out a feeling of strength.

Some single animal sculptures are also impressive. One stone carving of a frog is made in green granite. Its texture, feel and shape are similar to that of a real frog.

Artless Craft

It is necessary to ask after seeing the above stone carvings why sculptural techniques from the Han Dynasty seem so crude and simplistic when compared with the elegant and delicate figures of the earlier Qin Dynasty. The fact is that there were many horse figures made during the Han Dynasty and many metal sculptures that inherited the realistic style of the Qin terracotta warriors and horses.

There is another famous representative sculpture of the Han Dynasty: The bronze statue of a Horse Stepping on a Swallow. The romantic image of the swallow sets off the power and strength of the horse, providing a rich imaginative experience for viewers. The stone carving technique is sophisticated and representative of the aesthetic considerations of the Han Dynasty.

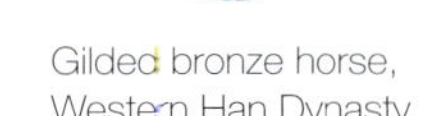
Gilded bronze horse, Western Han Dynasty.

Horse Stepping on a Swallow, Eastern Han Dynasty.

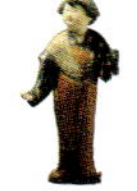

Skillful, but not exquisite

The stone carvings of the tomb of Huo Qubing adopted a realistic technique and abstract style. When craftsmen carved the figures of animals, they used the natural characteristics of material to reflect those of the animals. The stone is carved based on its nature. It is skillful but not refined with Chinese traditional aesthetic values, in sharp contrast with the aesthetic values of the late Qing Dynasty.

Chinese culture is reserved, undemonstrative and gentle and has been so for more than a thousand years. The reserved beauty of the tomb of Huo Qubing is like beautiful jade hiding in a stone. Although it is not exquisitely carved, it contains the profound philosophy of great art.

Carved stone animals in the Eastern Han Dynasty

The carved stone animals that guard mausoleums are outstanding representatives of the stone carvings from the Han Dynasty. These carved stone animals are fantastical. They resemble tigers but are not tigers. They are ferocious, strong, vigorous and powerful. A piece of stone carving unearthed in Xianyang, Shaanxi Province, in 1959 is 105cm tall and 159cm long. The stone animal has its chin up and chest out with two eyes that are wide open. It is roaring and looking around superciliously. The complete sculpture is forceful and powerful. The waving of the body gives a feeling of vitality.

These types of carved stone animals guarded the mausoleums and were always in pairs. Two such animals stand in front of the tomb of a procurator from the Eastern Han Dynasty. The words *tianlu* ("god blessing you") and *bixie* ("avoidance of evil") are

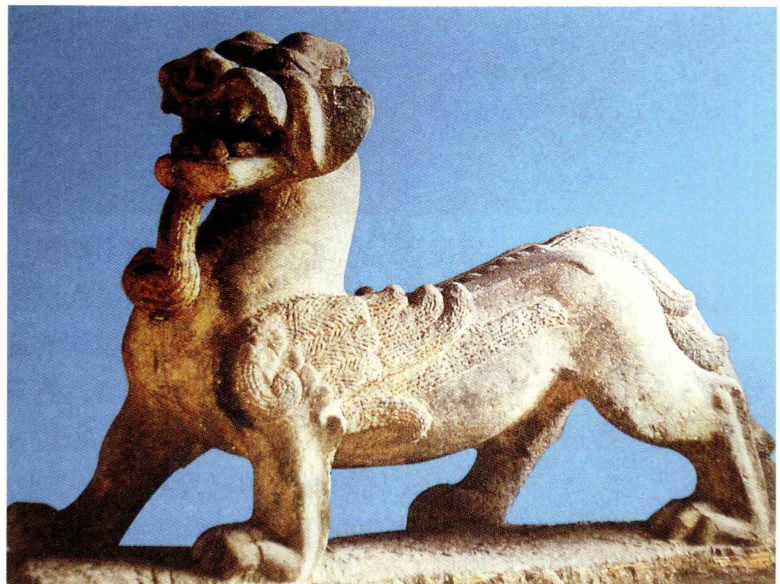

Bixie (avoidance of evil), Eastern Han Dynasty.

engraved on their arms. Ouyang Xiu (1007–1072) an outstanding writer and historian from the Northern Song Dynasty mentioned these two words in a book and later generations used the same words to name imaginative wild animals. The carved stone animals from the Eastern Han Dynasty are filled with vitality, power and wisdom, and had a far reaching impact on decorative stone carvings from mausoleums of later ages. Taken together, sculptural arts from the Han Dynasty contain important and inherent characteristics of traditional Chinese culture.

Introduction of Buddhism and the Blending of Cultures

Large-scale Grotto Images

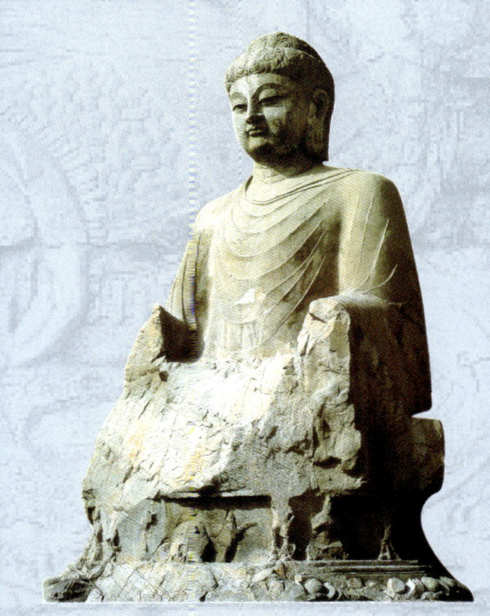

Buddhism was introduced into China during the Eastern Han Dynasty. Buddhist art spread widely during the Northern and Southern Dynasties and had a far-reaching impact on the development of society. Buddhist art thrived in terms of sculpture, painting and industrial arts during the Northern and Southern Dynasties, during which Buddhist images occupied a leading position. Chinese sculptural art expanded unprecedentedly during this period and surpassed the Qin and Han dynasties in terms of quantity, scale, artistry and spiritual dimension.

Similar to Buddhist architecture, Chinese Buddhist sculpture falls largely into three types: Grotto images, temple sculptures and image steles, as well as some small scale Buddha and Bodhisattva images. Grotto images were widely engraved after Buddhism entered China. The engraving of Buddhist grottoes had an immediate connection with Indian Buddhist grottoes. During the Wei, Jin, the Northern and Southern dynasties, craftsmen cut caves and sculpted Buddhist images in quiet mountain areas. These caves were the ashram of Buddhism. Many Buddhist grottoes can be found in western areas of China such as Xinjiang and Gansu. The stone in these places is soft and difficult to carve. Therefore, the grotto images are clay sculptures. In the central plains of China, the stone is hard and sharp, good for engraving. Therefore, the famous Longmen Grottoes and Yungang Grottoes can be found here. But these grottoes have few fresco paintings.

The carving of Chinese Buddhist grottoes began during the second year of Jianyuan of the Eastern Jin Dynasty (366). Buddhist grottoes were distributed in Xinjiang, Gansu, Ningxia, Shaanxi, Shanxi, Henan, Hebei, Shandong, Liaoning, Jiangsu, Sichuan, Guangxi, Yunnan and other places from west to east following transportation routes at the time.

The excavation of grottoes reached its peak between the Northern Wei and the Sui and Tang dynasties. After the Tang

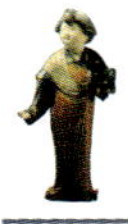

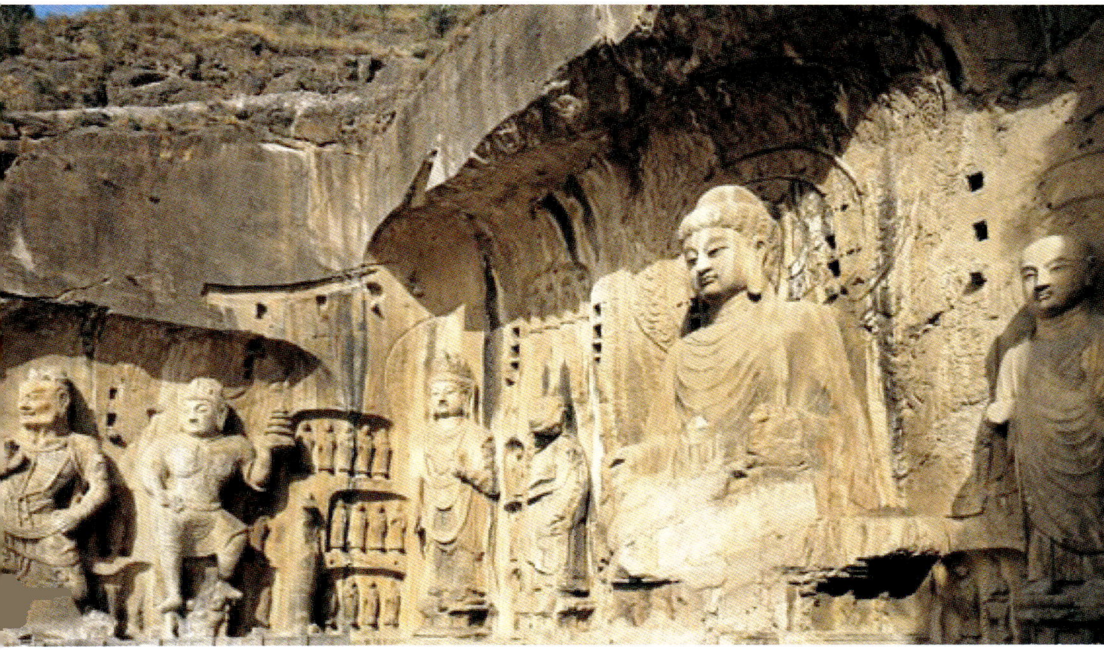

Statues in Fengxian Temple, Longmen, Tang Dynasty.

Dynasty, a few grotto temples and Buddhist grottoes were constructed. With the spread of Buddhism, Buddhist images gradually incorporated aspects of Ghandaran Buddhist Arts and combined them with the Buddhist side of Chinese culture. Among several hundred remaining grottoes, Dunhuang Mogao Grottoes, Maijishan Grottoes, Longmen Grottoes and Yungang Grottoes are collectively known as the four big grottoes. They are best known for their scale and historical value as well as their sculptures.

Mogao Grotto images

Located on the eastern slope of Rattling Sand Mountain (*Mingshashan*) southeast of Dunhuang County, Gansu Province, the Mogao Grottoes (also known as the Thousand Buddha Caves) is one of three noted grottoes in China. The complex contains the earliest carved grotto in the country. No other grottoes took so long to build or have such rich content. The grottoes preserve Buddhist images from the Wei, Jin, Northern and Southern dynasties to the Yuan Dynasty. The works of the Buddhist images lasted for nearly 900 years and the fresco paintings are nearly a thousand years old. The Mogao grottoes have 492 caves with florid murals and more than 2,000 painted statues. The study of the murals, statues and other cultural relics of the Dunhuang Grottoes has become an international subject of study called "Dunhuangology."

The Mogao Grottoes in the Wei, Jin, Northern and Southern Dynasties

The main part of the grottoes is the statues, not the murals or colored paintings, and they are magnificent. Murals and colored drawings enrich the themes of the statues. The Buddha and Bodhisattva images during the Wei, Jin, the Northern and Southern Dynasties have strong bodies, rounded faces and high Roman noses. Their posture is a bit stiff and unnatural. The design of the clothing is decorative. Only the neckline and the edge of the clothes are realistically carved.

All these characteristics were adopted from Indian Ghandaran images. For example, the Buddha and Bodhisattva images are obviously influenced by the Ghandaran style. In time, however, sculpture and facial appearance began to show the characteristics of Chinese people. In the No.259 Pit, the Buddha at the right niche is generally known as the "oriental Mona Lisa" because its smile seems to change subtly and unpredictably like Leonardo Da Vinci's *Mona Lisa*. Buddhist images from the period show the wisdom, mercy and joyousness of the Buddha and Bodhisattva, an improvement and progress in sculptural art.

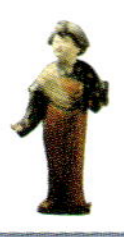

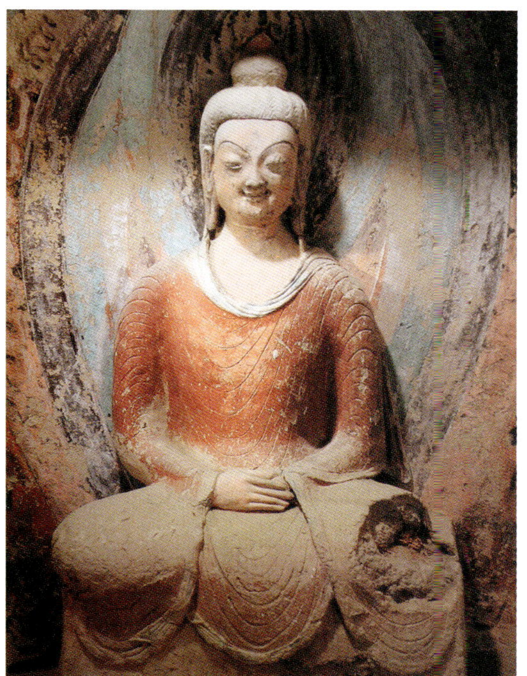

A single Buddha, No. 259 of Dunhuang Mogao grottoes, Northern Wei.

The earliest images of the Buddha and Bodhisattva come from foreign countries—most believe the originals were the images from the Kushan Empire (c. first to third centuries) in Gandhara. Buddhist scriptures have strict regulations on sculpture, proportion, posture, gesture, clothing and ornaments. Many changes were later made to make Buddhist art more acceptable to Chinese people, who had difficulty in accepting the exotic styles and images. The images were sculpted in compliance with Buddhist scriptures but with Chinese facial features. The combination used during the Wei and Jin dynasties is not natural but a little stiff.

In Buddhist images, the sculpture of Buddha Maitreya (the Buddha of the future) requires different skills from those used in other Buddha images. It was creative with obvious Chinese characteristics. The creativity is mainly reflected in the sitting position of the Buddha. In ancient India, sitting Buddhas were kneeling and sitting, but the Buddha Maitreya from the Wei and Jin dynasties always sits with two legs crossed. Rulers of the Xianbei Nationality considered this a noble sitting position. In the No.275 Pit, the main Buddha is the tall Maitreya and there are four others in the niches.

The prevalence of belief in Maitreya during this period can be attributed to two factors. First, from 266 to 313, Dharmaraksa, a

Yueh-Chih Buddhist monk, was the first to translate the Lotus Sutra into Chinese. He translated more than 150 pieces of scripture and helped disseminate belief in Maitreya. Second, Maitreya represented a vision for the future. Belief in Maitreya helped overcome the difficult circumstances and chaos caused by war.

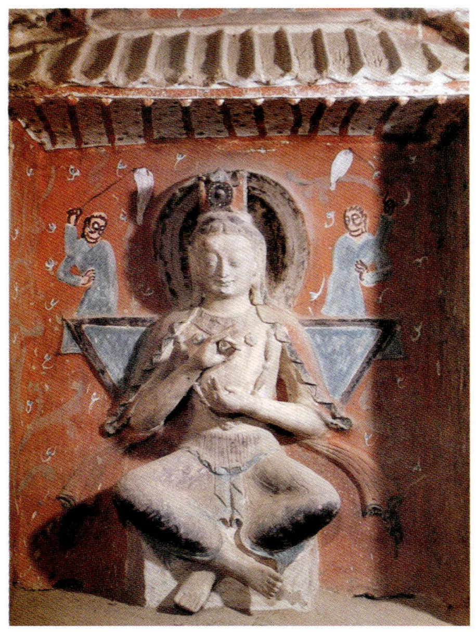

Legs-crossed Maitreya Bodhisattva, No. 275 of Dunhuang Mogao Grottoes, Northern Liang.

Buddhist images gradually incorporated Chinese features, as evidenced by the clothing of the Buddha. The process of Chinese localization among the Xianbei ethnic nationality accelerated the localization of Buddhist art. Indian gauze was replaced by the dress of an ancient Chinese scholar. The Buddhas wear crossed collars with a double-breasted cassock, which give them a kingly manner. The images of Buddha and Bodhisattva shifted from the robust and tall and developed an elegant Chinese appearance, valued during the Wei, Jin, and the Northern and Southern dynasties.

The number of grottoes created during the Wei, Jin, the Northern and Southern dynasties is far less than that created during the Tang Dynasty, and the sculptures are not as high in quality as those of the Tang.

The Mogao Grottoes in the Tang Dynasty

The Dunhuang Grottoes are the biggest of the Tang Dynasty grottoes. More than 670 statues from the Tang Dynasty were preserved in these caves.

The image groups of the Mogao Grottoes are usually made of one Buddha, two Buddhist saints, two Bodhisattvas, two heavenly kings and two warrior attendants. The Buddha images are usually rounded and elegant, sitting on the lotus throne, with spiral-shaped coiled hair and wearing cassocks. The clothes were well matched with the curves of the body. Each Buddha image has its own characteristics. Some are wise, some are charitable, some are thoughtful and others seem simple and cheerful. The most noticeable Buddha image is the sleeping statue of Nirvana Buddha in the No.158 Cave. It shows the death of Sakyamuni. The statue is lying down with two eyes half closed. It is quiet and peaceful, showing the highest possible and most desirable religious state: nirvana.

The images of Bodhisattvas and heavenly maidens are reminiscent of young girls. Most are plump, elegant, dignified and reserved; they look enchanting but have a sense of dignity, which shows the ideal of feminine beauty during the Tang

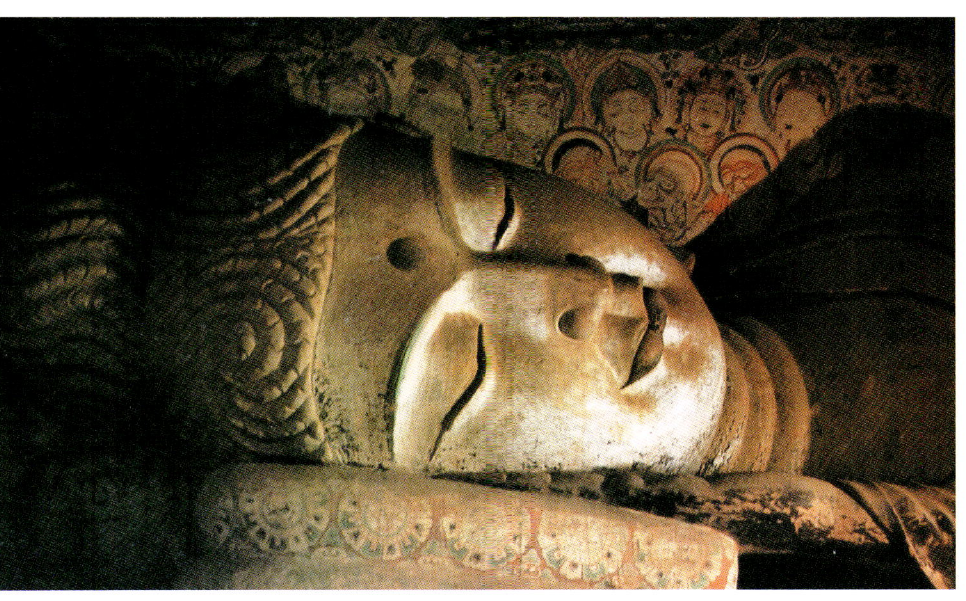

Statue of Nirvana Buddha, No. 158 of Dunhuang Mogao Grottoes, Tang Dynasty.

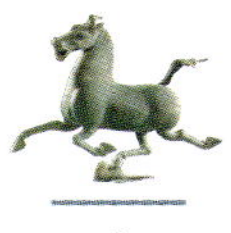

Dynasty. The images of Bodhisattva from the Tang Dynasty retained the Indian tradition. During the mid- and late Tang Period, Bodhisattva images seemed slim and had a common touch that was full of a sense of reality in daily life.

The images of Buddhist Saints were usually those of a young man and an old man. The elder is the Kasyapa Buddha and the younger is Ananda. Buddhist scriptures set out fewer limitations on statues of Buddhist saints and as a result these statues have varied and distinctive features. For example, the elder Kasyapa Buddha is sculpted as the image of a knowing high priest (in the No.45 Cave), and the young Ananda is a juvenile image that seems lost in thought.

Besides the dignified Buddha images, kind Bodhisattvas and thoughtful Buddhist Saints, the heavenly kings and Buddha's warrior attendants are also strong and brave or have ferocious facial expressions. The images of the heavenly king are mighty and full of awe; the Buddha's warrior attendants have bare upper bodies with strong muscle and are full of strength. Two heavenly kings in the No.46 Cave are images of two western people, highlighting the close connection between the Tang Dynasty and the west. The images of warrior attendants in the No.194 Cave show the excellent sculptural technique of the mid-Tang Dynasty. Body structures comply with modern anatomical

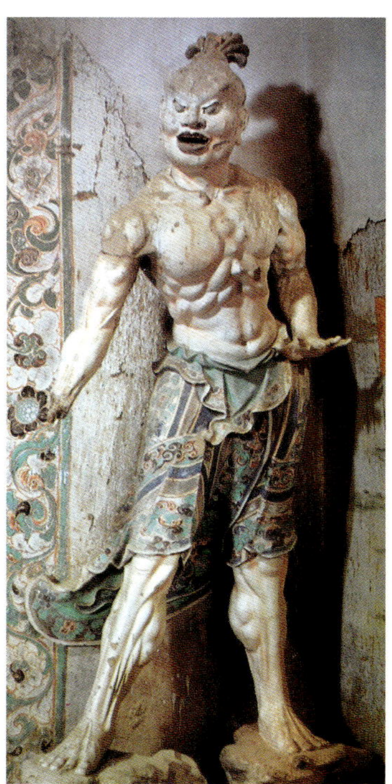

Statue of a muscleman, No. 194 of Dunhuang Mogao Grottoes, Tang Dynasty.

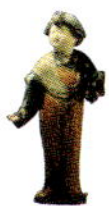

knowledge. The changes in the muscles and bones in the legs are strong and robust with very realistic appearence.

Statues in the Mogao Grottoes from the Tang Dynasty and others in the temple are not just standalone statues. The group is important as a whole. Everything works despite their independence and the group does not hinder the overall sense of the individual works. Different artists working in different styles produce different works, and thus images of the same figure do not have the same appearance and ethos. Expressions and postures are not identical. The images from the Dunhuang Grottoes give a good clear of the wealth of Tang Dynasty Buddhism, which not only impacted the Central Plains but, along with Tibetan Buddhism, had an influence in Japan, Korea, Vietnam and other countries.

Maijishan Grotto Images

Maiji Mountain is about 45km southeast of Tianshui City, Gansu Province. Although the mountain is only 142m tall, it is shaped like a haystack so it gets its name from the Chinese word for haystack, *maiji*. The excavation of Maiji Mountain started during the Sixteen Kingdoms Period (after 386) and continued through the Northern Wei, Western Wei, Northern Zhou, Sui, Tang, the Five Dynasties, Song, Yuan, Ming and Qing Dynasties. More than 7,000 clay Buddhist statues and stone carvings were done over 1,500 years. The stone here is similar to that of Dunhuang, which is difficult to carve. Therefore, many works are painted clay sculptures as stone carvings here required stone to be transported from elsewhere. Clay sculptures are popular in China because they can be preserved for more than a thousand years after firing.

The sculptural style found in the Maijishan grottoes has an obvious tendency towards the unreligious. Except for the

Ghandaran style early works, most Buddha images are amiably bowing their heads. Han Dynasty characteristics are visible in the figures and clothes of the statues. The Buddha and Boddhisattva images are beautiful with kind smiles. Their clothing is not restricted by Buddhist rites. The early clay sculptures in the Maijishan grottoes are more skillful; they are more simple and elegant and better suit the traditional aesthetic values of the Chinese people.

The Buddha and Boddhisattva images from the Northern Dynasties are elegant and pretty, while the Buddha's warrior attendants are strong and powerful. Two warrior attendants in the No. 122 Cave are outstanding works. One has his hair bristled up in anger. Another is grotesque and contrasts clearly with the images of Buddha and Boddhisattva, another universal rule of the sculptures of the grottoes.

Due to the long time they took to construct, the Buddha images of Maijishan show various changes. No.13 Grotto has the most eye-catching cliff-side image, at the center of eastern cliff. The main Buddha statue is more than 15m high and is made of clay. The Buddha is dignified. It has two ears and one Boddhisattva at either side. The facial expressions of the Bodhisattvas are vivid. No.4 Grotto, also known as *Sanhualou* or *Shangqi* Buddha Pavilion, is the highest, largest and the most beautiful grotto of the Maijishan complex. The grotto was built at the highest layer of

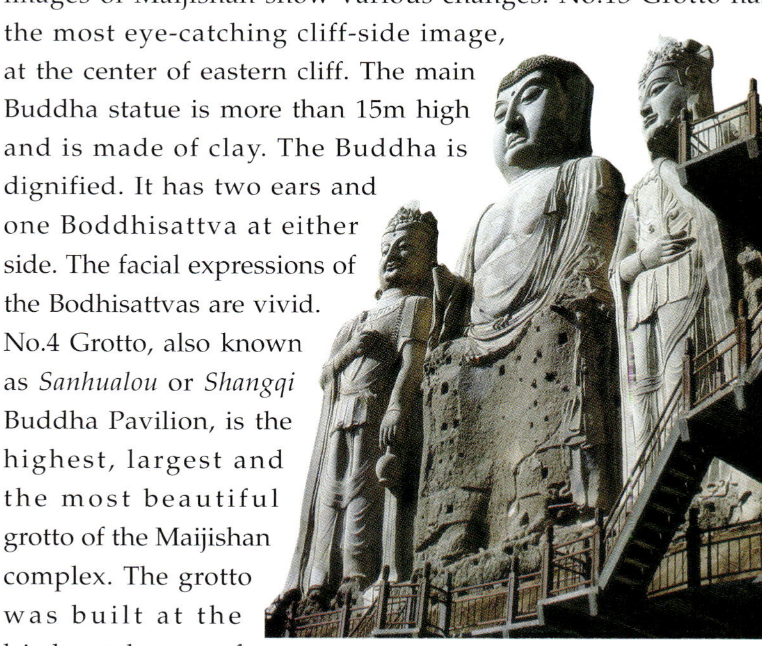

Cliffside statues, No. 13 shrine of Maiji Mountain Grottoes, Sui Dynasty.

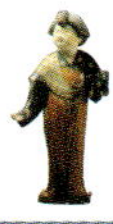

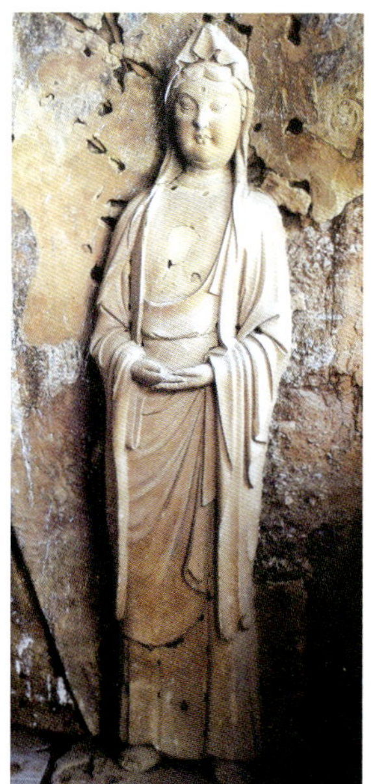

Standing statue of Kwan-yin Bodhisattva, Left wall of No. 165 of Maiji Mountain Grottoes, Song Dynasty.

the east cliff of Maiji Mountain in the Northern Zhou Dynasty (557–581). It was rebuilt in the Sui, Tang, Song and Ming dynasties.

No.165 Grotto is famous for its sculptures in the style of the Song Dynasty. The extant sculptures were constructed during the Northern Song. The Bodhisattva statue sits on the throne cross-legged with one attendant on each side. These Bodhisattva statues and attendants have round faces with long curved eyebrows, narrow eyes, small and delicate mouths and dignified appearances. The muscles on their faces are full of a sense of truth. The hairline on the attendants is extremely thin. The skin is finely textured and the drapery is refined and skillful. This could be considered the classic work of the Song Dynasty.

As a whole, the Maijishan Grottoes are elegant, simple and closer to Chinese traditional culture than the Dunhuang grottoes. Many Bodhisattva images look like the young girls from the northwest, while some statues reflect the humane ideology of Confucius.

Yungang Grotto Images

The Yungang Grottoes punctuate the north cliff of Wuzhou Mountain, Datong City, Shanxi Province. The area was excavated along 1km from east to west and includes 53 caves and over 51,000 stone statues.

The famous monk Tan Yao created the Tanyao Five Grottos (Caves 16–20) during the Northern Wei Dynasty (460–470). Other caves were built after the eighteenth year (494) of the Taihe reign of the Northern Wei, more than 1,500 years ago. The caves can be divided into early, middle and late caves based on when they were carved.

The early Five Caves are full of power and grandeur. They are dignified and simple in the style of *Xiyu*, a western region in ancient China.

The grottoes from the middle period are delicate and refined, complicated and varied with Chinese characteristics. The sculpting of the faces and clothes of the Buddha has a tendency towards realism. The typical dress of "loose clothes and broad strap" appeared and became popular in the Central Plains of China. The Buddha image is smaller and is more amiable. These practices in sculpture better suit the characteristics of Chinese culture.

Loose Clothes and Broad Strap

The phase "loose clothes and broad strap" originated from the *History of Han Dynasty* by Ban Gu of the Eastern Han Dynasty. Both "loose" and "broad" have the sense of broadness. "Loose clothes and broad strap" means "wearing a loose robe and broad strap," and it was the common costume of the ancient Confucian scholars. It was extraordinarily popular in the Wei and Jin dynasties. The basic form creates a sense of freedom and ease, and is also unique and free from vulgarity.

During the later period, the statues are beautifully created and slim. They are moderate in size and closer to real features. The images begin to show features of people from the Central Plains. During this period, Buddhist grotto excavation was transferred to Longmen of Luoyang. Chinese Buddhist art began to show its own characteristics and these images ensured the spread of Buddhism.

It is possible to trace the historical path from the Indian and Central Asian Buddha to the Chinese Buddha. Buddha statues were gradually secularized in China. In terms of engraving skills, they combined the skills

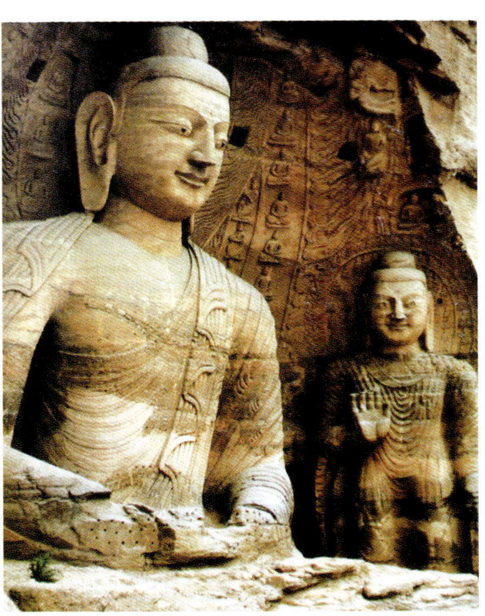

Statue of sitting Sakyamuni Buddha, No. 20 of Yungang Grottoes, Northern Wei.

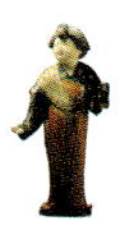

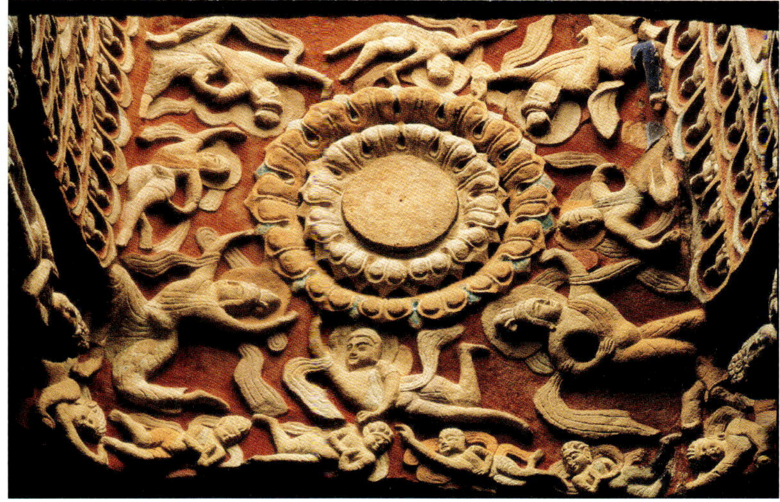

Sculpture Flying Apsaras, Top of No. 10 of Yungang Grottoes, Northern Wei.

of the Chinese Qin and Han Dynasty and Gandhara art to create unique artworks, an important step in the history of Chinese sculpture.

Longmen Grotto Images

Located south of Luoyang, Henan Province, the Longmen Grottoes are concentrated on the east and west cliffs of the Yishui River (known as *Yique* in ancient times). The grottoes were started around the year 494 when Emperor Xiaowen of the Northern Wei Dynasty moved the capital to Luoyang. They were built continuously throughout 400 years until the Northern Song Dynasty. The area is 1,000m from north to south where there are over 2,345 holes and niches and 100,000 statues. Most of these works are from the Northern Wei Dynasty and the flourishing age of the Tang Dynasty.

Lots of historical material concerning art, music, religion, calligraphy, medicine, costume and architecture is kept in the

Longmen Grottoes. During the Northern Wei Dynasty, the excellent representatives of the Longmen Grottoes were the Binyang Grotto and its internal decoration. During the Tang Dynasty, the gigantic Buddha sculpture in the Fengxian Temple was the biggest and best part of the Longmen Grottoes. It represented the highest sculptural achievement of the Tang Dynasty.

Binyang Grotto

The Binyang Grotto is one of the most representative grottoes of the Longmen Grottoes. It is divided into the North Binyang Cave, Middle Binyang Cave and South Binyang Cave. Started during the Northern Wei Dynasty, the cave was not completed until the Tang.

The Middle Binyang Grotto is the representative work of the Northern Wei. In this cave, the entire design is coherent in thought and stylistically uniform. The exquisite decoration echoes the solemn Buddha statues, showing the magnificence and mystery of Buddhism. The carving of the whole cave engenders a feeling of sublimity, symmetry and orderliness. A Buddhist fairyland was engraved including beautiful lotus and vines on the ground, the smooth garments of Buddha and Bodhisattvas, gorgeous light and clouds and the Flying Grottoes.

The statue of Sakyamuni, the major one in the grotto, has big eyes and a rounded nose. The statute is slim and kindly. The body is well proportioned. The Buddha and Bodhisattva images in the cave are slim and elegant with "angel" sleeves. This style influenced the Buddha images of the late Northern Wei period. As the center of the Central Plains culture, Longmen had notable differences from the artistic style of the Yungang grottoes. The bold and generous style reflected in Yungang art was replaced by the delicate and amiable style of the Longmen grottoes, another example of how China adopted Buddhist art.

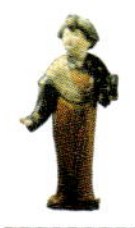

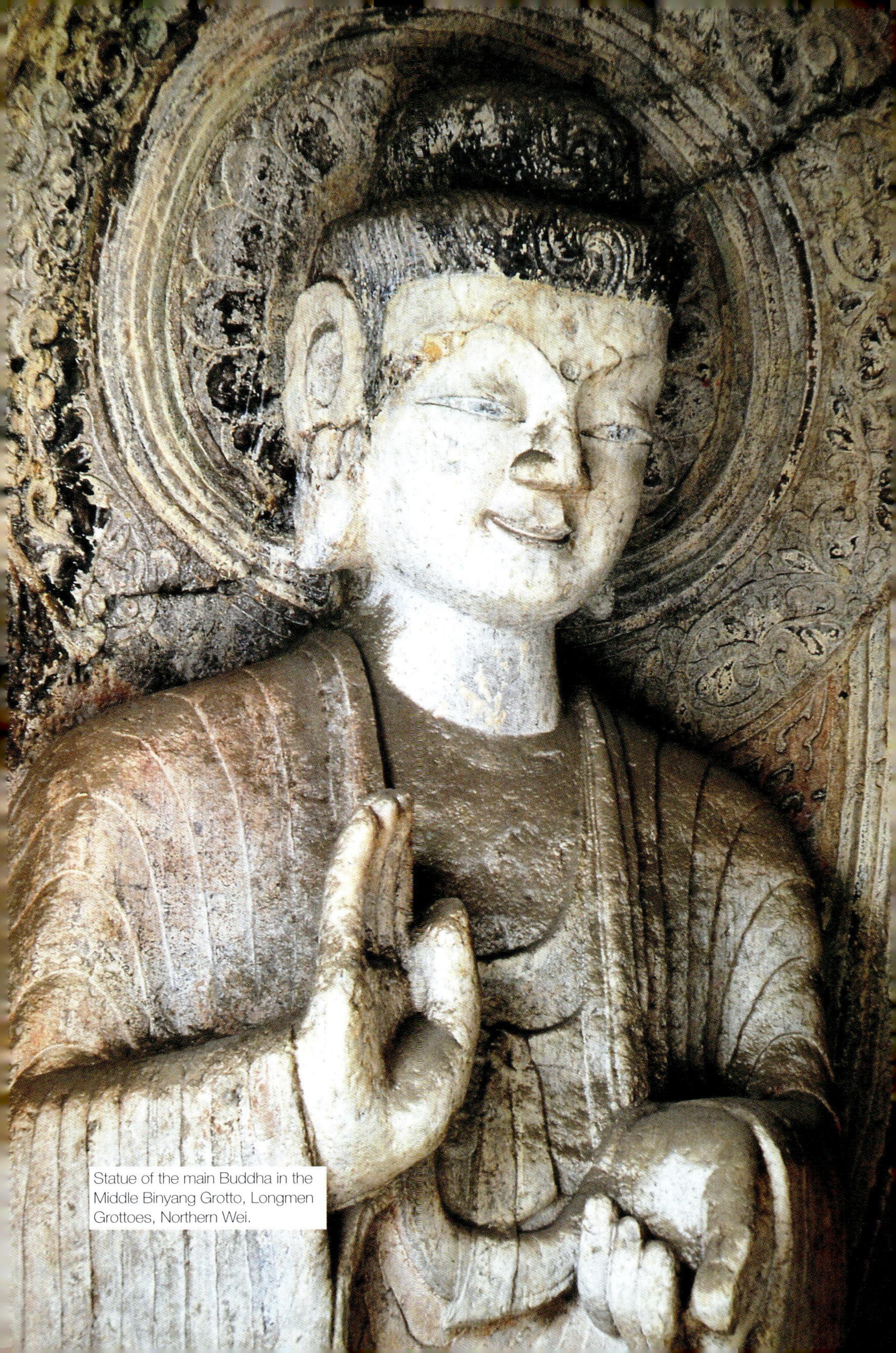

Statue of the main Buddha in the Middle Binyang Grotto, Longmen Grottoes, Northern Wei.

Fengxian Temple

The Fengxian Temple was built during the Tang Dynasty. It is the largest grotto in the Longmen Temple. The grotto was started during the reign of Empress Wu Zetian (624–705). The faces of the statues are large and their expressions quiet and kind, hinting at Buddhist tendencies in Tang Dynasty art.

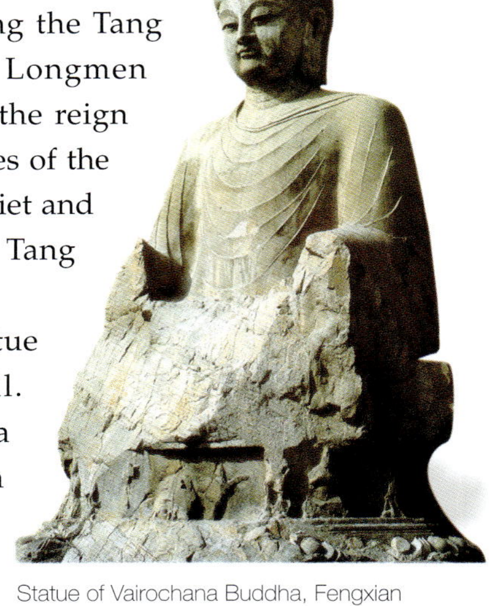

Statue of Vairochana Buddha, Fengxian Temple, Longmen Grottoes, Tang Dynasty.

The most impressive figure is the statue of Vairocana Buddha. It is 17.14m tall. The Buddha has a well-filled figure, a sacred and kindly expression and an elegant smile. The drapery is smoothly designed. The statue is the best example of a Buddha sculpture from the Tang Dynasty.

The layout of the Fengxian Temple is also the best among the Buddha sculptures of the Tang Dynasty. The two attendants on both sides of the Vairocana Buddha, Ananda and Kasyapa Buddha, are gentle and religious with divine grace and a benevolent appearance. The guardian king sits on the throne with a martial and cautious expression; the warrior attendants have big staring eyes and appear mighty. They give a strong sense of integrity.

China's large-scale grotto statues were sculpted during the Wei, Jin, Sui and Tang dynasties. Although Buddhists were regularly persecuted, grotto statues still prospered and matured while developing richer content. Following their introduction into China they started combining aspects from northern nomad nationalities and characteristics of the culture of the Central Plains as the Chinese gradually absorbed western Buddhism.

The Dignity of the Kingdom of Heaven

Sculptures of Emperors' Tombs and Pottery Sculptures

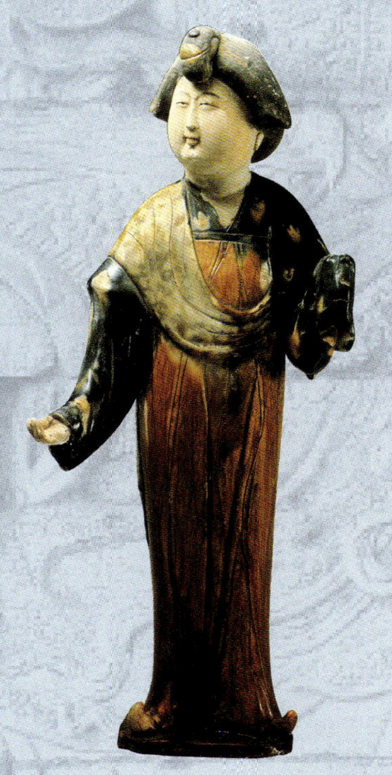

In ancient China, the deaths of emperors or their relatives were important events. Emperors took many of their belongings into their graves, a custom similar to that of the ancient pharaohs in Egypt. One important difference, however, was that Chinese emperors did not hope to retain their bodies to continue their life after death. They did not make corpses into mummies, but paid attention to the continuity of spiritual life.

The construction of large tombs for emperors and the pottery figures inside them can be traced back to the Shang and Zhou dynasties. The Qin Terracotta Warriors and Horses discussed above reflect an important aspect of this burial culture. From the Han Dynasty onwards, tombs built above ground became more important. The catacombs of emperors include many objects, pottery figures, and martial implements placed outside the coffin chambers showing the lordliness and prestige of emperors and nobles. The carvings on the tomb of Huo Qubing are similar to the carvings on the ground but their meaning is different from the stone carvings of the emperors' tombs: The former is more narrative while the latter's aim is to protect the tomb. Stone carvings were not used to protect tombs until the Eastern Han Dynasty. Most of the carvings that have survived are those in front of the tombs of magistrates.

The sculpture in emperors' tombs made bigger strides during the Northern and Southern Dynasties, especially the Southern. It developed important patterns and reached the height of its power and splendor in the Tang Dynasty.

Guard beast figures in the Wei, Jin, Northern and Southern Dynasties

Although the Qin and Han dynasties represent the first peak of construction of emperors' tombs, most of them were underground. Above ground stone carvings did not appear until the Han Dynasty and became predominant during the Northern and Southern Dynasties.

The funeral system of the Wei, Jin, Northern and Southern dynasties was similar to that of the Han Dynasty but it had gradually formed the common practice of using large-scale stone carvings to protect the tombs. The tombs included tombstones and huge stone beasts (*tianlu*, *kylin* and *bixie*).

The *kylin* and *bixie* were based on mythological animals but their body shapes were made bigger and are more ferocious, representing the style of the period. The Southern Dynasties refers to a series of regimes in southern China from about the fifth to the sixth century, and includes the Liu, Song, Southern Qi, Liang and dynasties. The Wei, Jin and Northern and Southern dynasties governed during a time of much chaos. Countries were created, others disappeared, some split up, some were broken. However, culture and art were full of vigor. During the Wei, Jin and Northern and Southern dynasties, ideology, culture and art combined and developed.

The stone carvings in tombs of the Southern Dynasty were carved for emperors and lords. As a result, they were carved exquisitely with huge bodies to symbolize dignity. Some thirty-three stone carvings have been found in Jiangsu Province, eleven of which were in Nanjing. These pieces could have been carved as far back as the Liu Song period, more than 1,500 years ago.

Most tombs of Chinese emperors face south. The stone carvings include stone beasts protecting the tomb, columns and monuments. The stone beasts are known as *tianlu*, *kylin* and *bixie*. They are tall with their heads raised proudly, mouths open and piercing eyes. Both sides of their stomachs are engraved with two wings with four crossed feet. The head of *tianlu* has a pair of horns, *kylin* has one horn and *bixie* none. *Tianlu*, also known as "heavenly deer," is a legendary divine beast and symbolizes the mandate of Heaven and a high position. *Kylin* (Chinese unicorn) is also auspicious. It first appeared early in the Warring States period, more than 2,500 years ago. These stone beasts protect the tombs and demonstrate the supreme authority of the owner. In tombs of the Southern Dynasty, *tianlu* and *kylin* were sculpted on the tombs of the emperors and *bixie* in the tombs of feudal lords, which were rigidly stratified.

In Jiangsu Province, there is a saying that Danyang is well known for *kylin* and Nanjing famous for *bixie*. The Xiao family, emperors of Qi and Liang, were buried in their hometown of Danyang. Their tombs were carved with *tianlu* and *kylin*. Most tombs of Qi and Liang feudal lords are in Nanjing and the trademark patterns of *bixie* are visible everywhere in the city. The city's emblem uses *bixie* as its major pattern.

Danyang's *tianlu* and *kylin* stone beasts are excellent examples of work found in imperial tombs from the Southern Dynasty, of which the Xiu'an, Yong'an and Jing'an tombs are the most representative tombs. The *kylin* is well preserved, attractive and tall.

The *bixie* in Nanjing looks strong and remarkable. The stone carvings of the tombs of Xiao Hong, Xiao Rong, Xiao Jing and Xiao Ji are the most vivid and representative. The *bixie* on the tomb of Xiao Hong is 3.2m long, 2.84m tall, and 3.35m at its waist. It weighs more than 15 tons. The *bixie* raises its head proudly with its long tongue out of its mouth and close to its chest, looking powerful and imposing.

The engraving technique is skillful and creates a new type of Chinese sculpture. The parts and the whole are very harmonious, showing a symmetrical beauty. In addition to the tomb-guarding beasts, tomb columns and tombstones were other types of stone carvings during the Southern Dynasty. The stone columns of Emperor Xiaojing, Emperor Jianwen of Liang and the Xiaoji tomb column in Jurong are the most famous.

There are only four stone columns left in Emperor Xiaojing's tomb. These columns are 6.50m high and have a diameter of 2.4m. They are divided into the base, body and cover of the

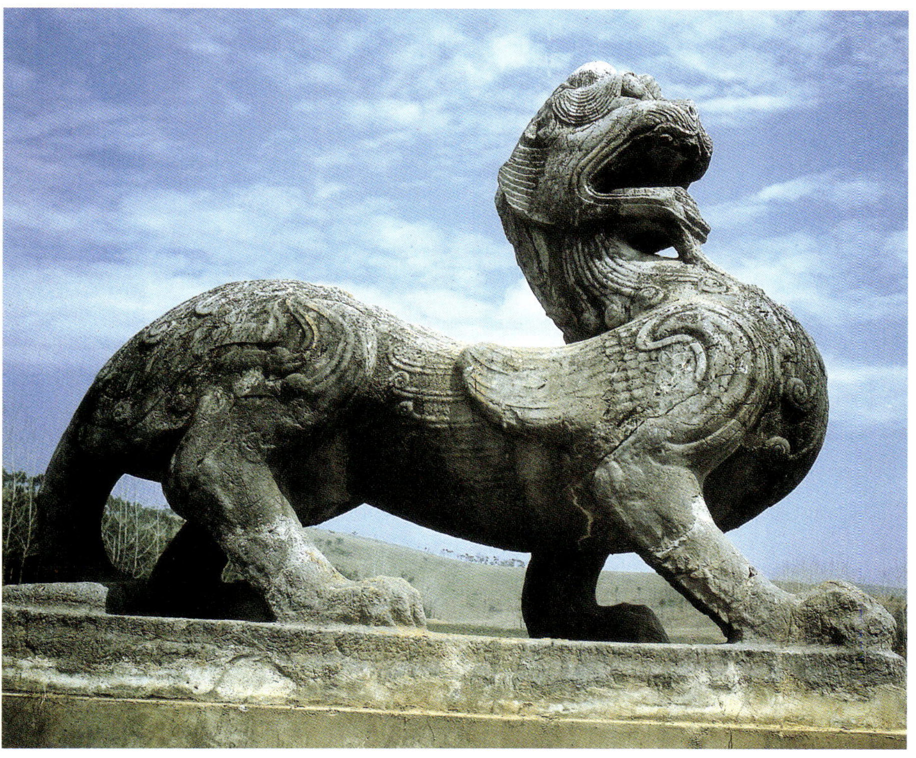

Xiao Daosheng, Emperor Jing of Qi, built the mausoleum to avoid evil, Southern Dynasty.

column. From the shape and decoration of stone columns of the Southern Dynasties, we can see that their style was indirectly affected by the cultures of ancient Greece and India. Exchanges between occidental and oriental countries were very extensive. The sculpture of the lotus throne was influenced by Buddhist art.

Most funeral objects in ancient Chinese coffin chambers are pottery figures. The pottery figures from the Northern Dynasties inherited a tradition of carving expressions from the Han Dynasty. The pottery figures include maids, musicians, warriors, troopers, bodyguards, servants, oxcarts, horses, camels and so on. The maid images are similar to the stone carvings of Buddha in their facial form, expression and posture. Female figures are pretty and slim, different from the plump beauty valued during the Tang Dynasty.

As a whole, sculptural art from the Wei, Jin, Northern and Southern dynasties forms a link between sculptures from the preceding Eastern and Western Han dynasties and the following Sui and Tang dynasties. There are more than twenty imperial tombs and stone statues near Nanjing, forming the body of stone sculpture work from the Northern and Southern Dynasties. The style of stone carvings in the imperial tombs from the Southern Dynasty discovered in Shaanxi, Henan, Hebei, Shanxi and other places is different from that of the Northern Dynasty. The unearthed stone tomb doors, *kistvaens* and *kistvaen* beds from the Northern Dynasty have great artistic value.

Imperial stone carvings in the Tang Dynasty

The Tang Dynasty brought with it the second tide of imperial tombs in Chinese history. The architectural style of these tombs further developed the form of the Wei, Jin, Northern and Southern Dynasties. The eighteen imperial tombs of the Tang Dynasty include the tomb of the empress Wu Zetian and those of another seventeen Tang emperors. They were buried on the northern bank of Weishui River, Shaanxi Province. They are known as "Eighteen Imperial Tombs at Guanzhong."

The tombs of Tang Dynasty emperors were built near mountains to take advantage of natural land formations. The Qianling Mausoleum, the tomb of the third Tang emperor, Li Zhi, and Empress Wu Zetian, are located on the peak of lofty Liangshan Mountain, about twenty or thirty meters higher than the mausoleums of the Qin and Han dynasties.

Qianling was originally enclosed by two walls. Investigation and prospecting uncovered the remains of the inner wall, four gates, a sacrificial hall and some corner parts of the outer wall. The southern gate was called *Zhu Que Men* (Rosefinch Gate), and it was a place to hold sacrificial ceremonies. Numerous buried tombs are distributed between the first and second gate. The number of tombs accompanying that of Tang Taizong (599–649) is 167.

The stone carvings and inscriptions in Tang Dynasty imperial tombs occupy an important place in the history of Chinese sculpture. The best of them are represented by the stone carvings of the Six Steeds of the Zhaoling Mausoleum, the Stone Lion at the Shunling Mausoleum and the *Shendao* (Sacred Way) Carved Stone of the Qianling Mausoleum.

The Six Steeds of the Zhaoling Mausoleum

Zhaoling is the mausoleum of Emperor Taizong of the Tang Dynasty, one of China's great emperors. Under his reign, the famous rule of Zhenguan emerged (Zhenguan is the name of his era), which laid a solid foundation for the economic and cultural development of the Tang Dynasty. The construction of Zhaoling is luxurious and majestic.

The six steeds represent the precious warhorses of Taizong, on which he fought battles for the unification of China. Emperor Taizong ordered that the stone carvings of the six steeds be put right beside the mausoleum when construction began to commemorate the battle achievements of these horses. The six horses are: Telebiao, Qingzhui, Shifachi, Saluzi, Quanmaoguo and Baitiwu.

The steeds had different colors, vigorous posture and extraordinary temperament. The last two stone horses were stolen and sold abroad in 1914 and are now on display at the University of Pennsylvania Museum. The posture, character and movement of the horses are depicted vividly through the relief sculpture technique.

The Stone Lion at the Shunling Mausoleum

The Shunling Mausoleum was the tomb of Yang Shi, the mother of Empress Wu Zetian. In the first year (670) of the Xianheng reign, Yang Shi died and was buried under the name of Li Wang. Wu Zetian granted her mother the title of Empress Xiao Minggao and named the tomb the Shunling Mausoleum after declaring herself empress. Twelve stone people, one stone

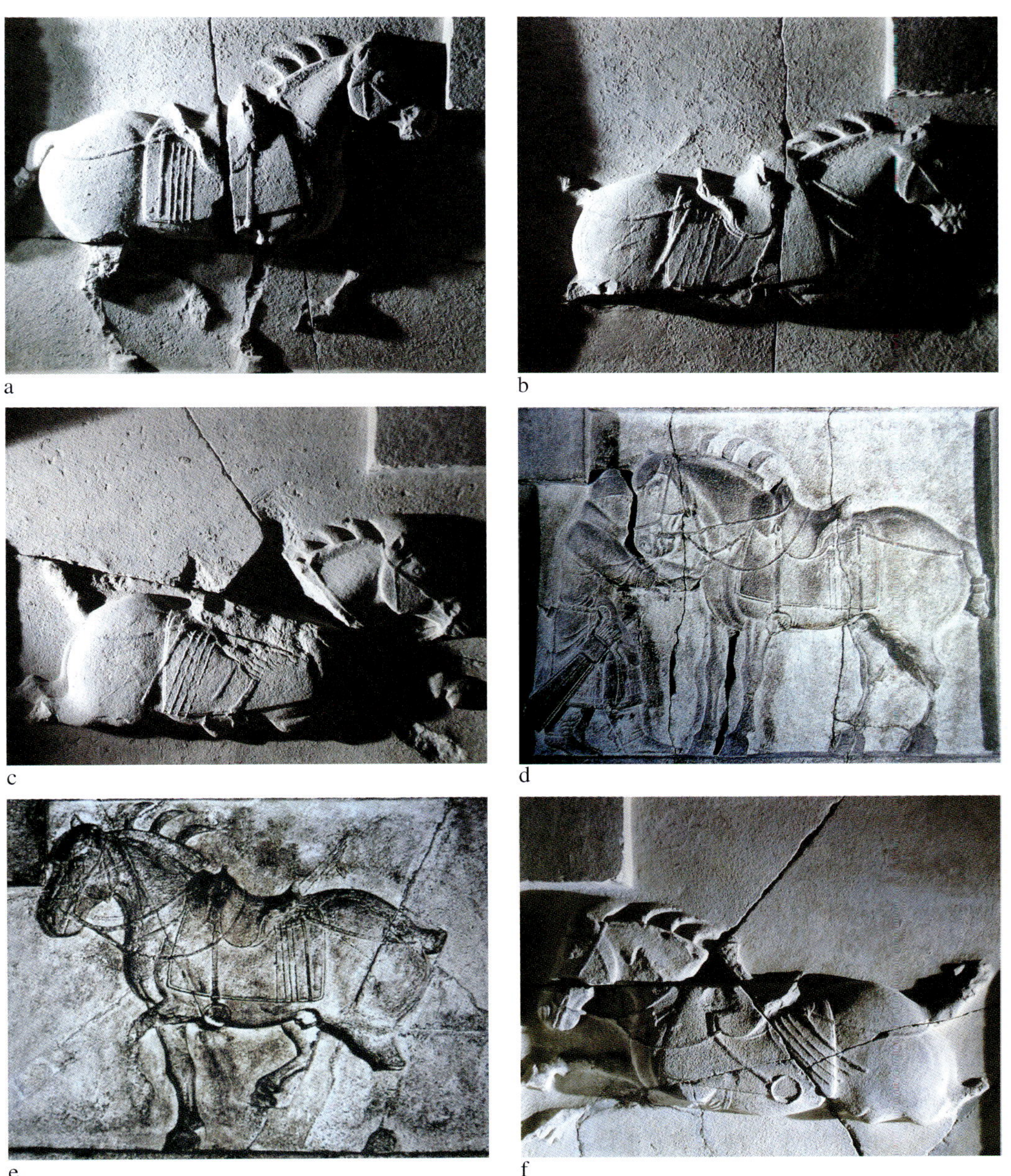

Six steeds at Zhaoling Mausoleum, Tang Dynasty.
a Telebiao b Qingzhui c Shifachi d Chaluzi and General Qiu Xinggong e Quanmaogua f Baitiwu

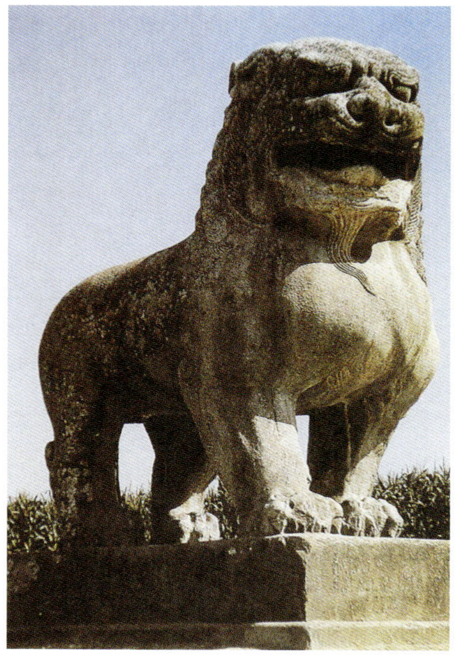

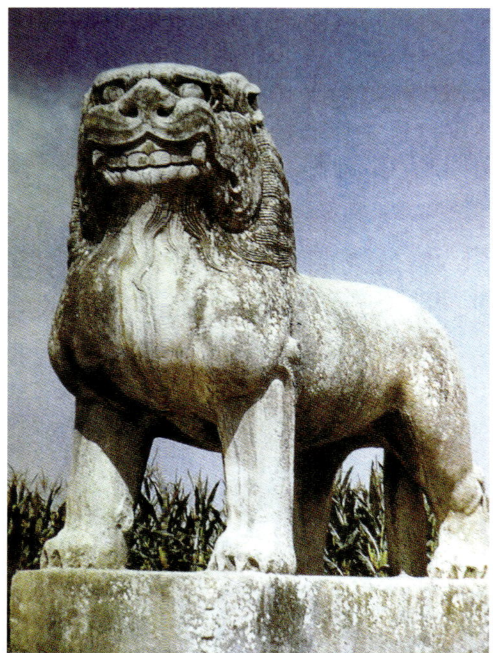

Stone lions at Shunling Mausoleum, Tang Dynasty.

sheep and a stone lion, one ornamental column and one lotus throne stand in front of the tomb. The east gate, west gate and north gate have a stone lion each. A pair of horses stands outside the north gate and a pair of walking lions and *tianlu* guard the south gate. The walking lion and stone *tianlu* are the masterpieces of the Shunling Mausoleum. The stone lion has a huge body, is 4m tall, with curly hair, extrusive eyes and a grand nose.

The Carved Stone of the Qianling Mausoleum

The Qianling Mausoleum of Emperor Gaozong of Tang (628–683), as well as the Zhou Dynasty usurper and China's first (and only) governing empress, Wu Zetian, is located 100km northwest

Tangcao

Tangcao, the vine grass, is thought to be endowed with the morals of continuity and serenity. With beautiful curves, it has undergone various changes with the passing of time and has been widely applied to all kinds of decoration, forming a special category in decorative patterns. The pattern, the typical decoration pattern in the Tang Dynasty, was very popular in the Sui and Tang dynasties, hence the name *Tangcao*.

from the peak of Liangshan Mountain. It is one of the best-preserved of the Eighteen Imperial Tombs and the most representative. A pair of ornamental columns, winged horses and stone horses, and ten pairs of civil and military officials stand at the second gate. In addition, a stele with no inscriptions and a stele recording the achievements of the emperor hang between the stone people and the third tower. Sixty-one stone statues depicting visitors were placed in front of the *Zhu Que Men*. These stone carvings enlarge the space of the mausoleum and reflect the dignity and supreme position of the emperors.

Prominent among the stone carvings of Qianling Mausoleum are a pair of winged horses. The winged horse or Pegasus is an auspicious animal. These sculptures, realistic in style, have highly decorative patterns. The curled patterns on the wings have the

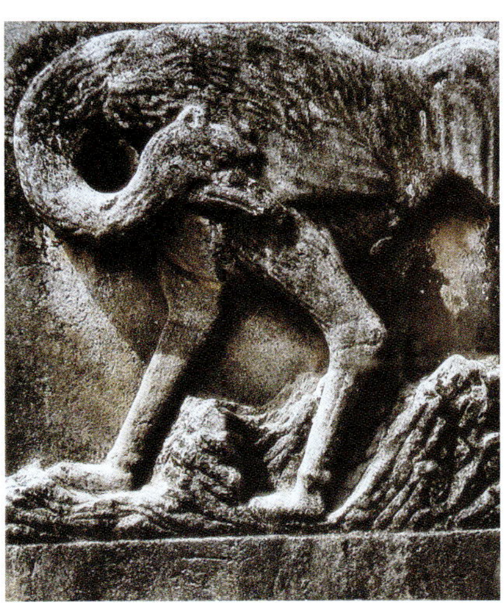

Ostrich at Qianling Mausoleum, Tang Dynasty.

similar features of *Tangcao*, a decorative pattern in the Tang Dynasty sculpture.

The postures and expressions of a large number of civil and military officials are the same, which seem a bit stiff from the individual point of view but together give the impression of standing out majestically.

A statue of an ostrich first appeared in the tomb of a Tang Dynasty emperor. In order to make it easier to carve the neck and legs, craftsman used the relief technique. The ostrich was considered a rare bird during the Tang Dynasty.

Pottery figures in Tang Dynasty tombs

The custom of burying objects was prevalent during the Tang Dynasty, and unearthed pottery sculptures are often found in Xi'an and Luoyang. Most of the tombs of nobles of the Tang are in these two places. In Shaanxi Province, more than 3,000 pottery sculptures have been excavated. More than 570 pottery men were found in the tomb of Princess Yongtai; more than 1,000 in the tomb of Prince Yide; about 600 in the tomb of Crown Prince Zhanghuai. These tricolor figurines are the most commonly seen sculptures. Tricolor pottery was the most important burial sculpture of the Tang Dynasty.

Grouped by category, pottery sculptures of the Tang Dynasty include female sculptures, male sculptures, musician and dancer sculptures, gods and spirits, and horse sculptures as well as sculptures of common domestic animals and so on.

Female sculptures: Female sculptures from the Tang Dynasty can be divided into three categories. The first is the typical Tang style, meaning that most women were plump, matching

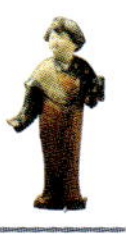

the aesthetic requirements of the Tang. A second female image has a round face but not a plump figure. The third kind is slim and pretty. The differences between female images are the result of the different status and position of people, times and regions. Female sculpture shows different styles in the Tang Dynasty's early, middle and late period and the Northern and Southern regions. The plump sculptures are noble women dressed in the style of the middle period. They can be usually found in Xi'an. Slim female sculptures show the elegant demeanor of southern China and appeared in the early Tang, still affected by the dress style of the Wei and Jin dynasties.

Tri-colored pottery standing female figures, Tang Dynasty.

Male sculptures: Male sculptures from Tang Dynasty tombs include warriors, flags bearers, weapons and attendants. The commonly seen attendants are *Kunlun* slaves and figurines of Hu people. Tang nobles employed a large number of people from different ethnic nations and west Asian people as their vassals, so such male sculptures are commonly seen in the tombs of the nobles of the Tang Dynasty.

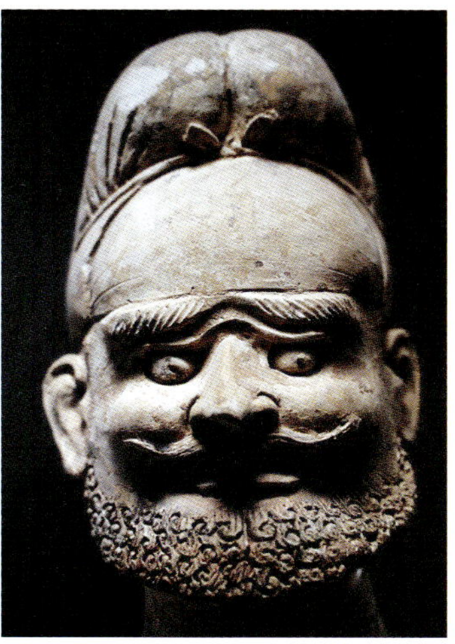

Head of a terracotta Tartar, Tang Dynasty.

Musicians and dancers: The sculptures of musicians and dancers are also important pottery pieces. They were made in the hopes of putting on a

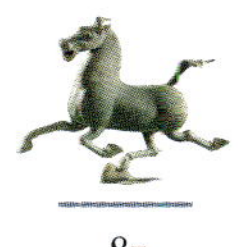

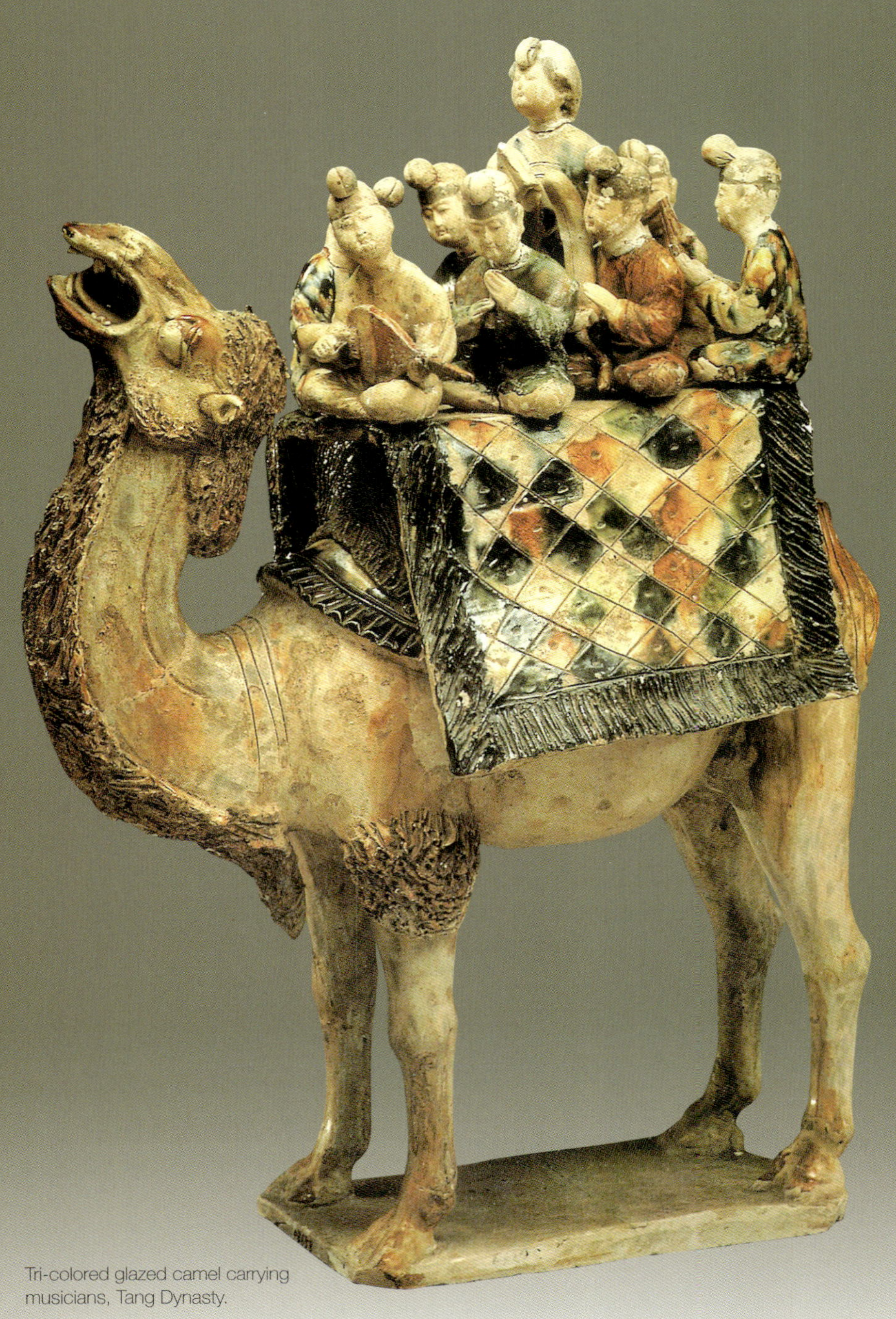

Tri-colored glazed camel carrying musicians, Tang Dynasty.

show of peace and prosperity for descendents. Ancient China had many kinds of music and dance. Therefore, sculptures of musicians and dancers found in the tombs are varied and very vivid.

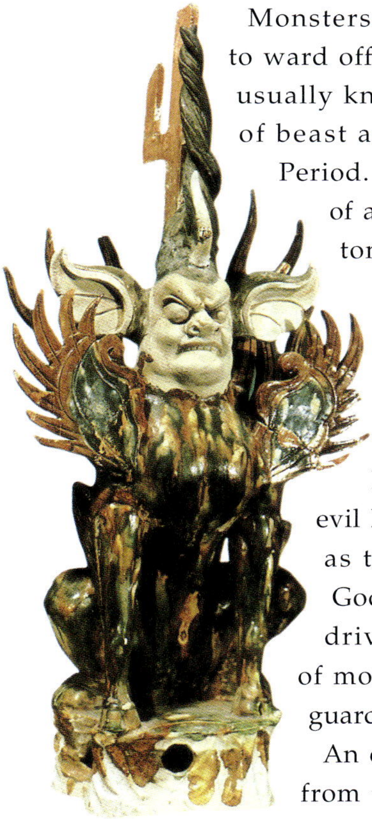

Monsters: Monster sculptures that were believed to ward off bad luck, evil and protect the dead were usually known as tomb-guarding beasts. This type of beast appeared as early as the Warring States Period. During the Northern Dynasty, sculptures of animals with human heads appeared. These tomb figures were more popular during the Sui and Tang dynasties, when various changes occurred. Tomb-guarding beasts during the Tang Dynasty made the biggest contribution to the development of images of animals with human heads from the Northern Wei Dynasty. They also developed evil half-human, half-animal images recognized as the evolution of the ancient Fangxiang God, meaning demons and monsters that can drive out evil spirits. People carved images of monsters squatting in the tombs. The tomb-guarding beasts always appeared in pairs.

Tri-colored tomb beast, Tang Dynasty.

An overall view of the stone carvings in tombs from the Wei, Jin to the Tang dynasties tells us much about the cultural atmosphere of that time. Sculptural art from the Tang shows the tolerance and moderation of that culture. It is a brief chronicle of that time.

The shape and structure of tombs from the Tang Dynasty changed during the Song Dynasty, which incorporated more common customs but lacked the beauty of power and vigor of the Tang. Stone carvings and pottery sculptures were rarely seen during the Yuan Dynasty. The Ming and Qing dynasties, although they continued to build tombs, did not better those of the middle Tang period.

Integration of Buddhism, Taoism and Confucianism

Temple Sculpture in the Song Dynasty

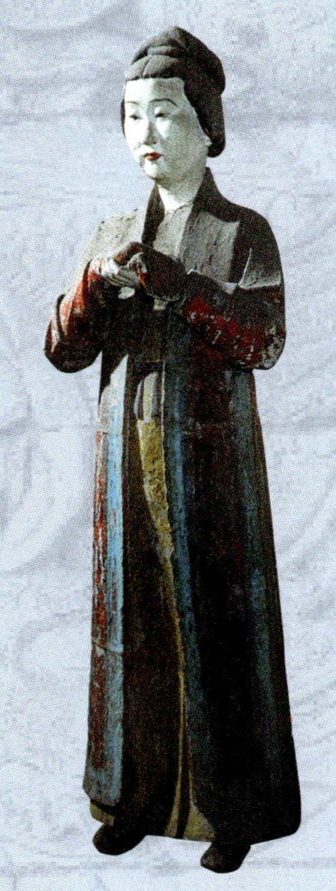

The establishment of the Northern Song Dynasty reunited a China that had been split for half century. After this, great changes took place in Chinese religion. One of the most distinctive characteristics was the change in Buddhism, Taoism and Confucianism from confrontation and repulsion to integration. From this time forward, Buddhism adopted a Chinese style and became an important part of the culture. The changes were a result of two factors. The first were changes in internal ideology and the spread of religion. Rulers accelerated the integration of the different religions to ensure social stability.

The integration of Buddhism, Taoism and Confucianism is not only reflected in the ideological realm, but also in art. Some temple sculptures of the Song and Yuan dynasties show such characteristics. Temples that combine the styles of Buddhism, Taoism and Confucianism, and grotto temples that show the union of the three religions appeared.

Painted Sculptures at Jinci Temple

At the foot of the Xuanweng Mountain, 25km southwest of Taiyuan, Shanxi Province, lies the famous Jinci Temple. The Jinci Temple was first built before the Northern Wei Dynasty (386–534) in memory of Shu Yu, the second son of Wuwang of the Zhou Dynasty. The temple was repaired and expanded several times through the Northern Qi, Sui, Tang, Song, Yuan, Ming and Qing dynasties.

Jinci Temple combines cultural relics and beautiful landscape. It is well known for the magnificent architecture and clay sculptures in the Goddess Temple. Jinci Temple combines styles from Buddhism, Taoism and Confucianism and reflects the union of three religions and the worship of multiple gods.

The Goddess Temple is the main building of the Jinci Temple. It faces east. It is majestic and large, forming a complex with other

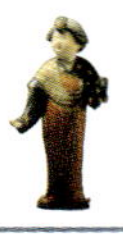

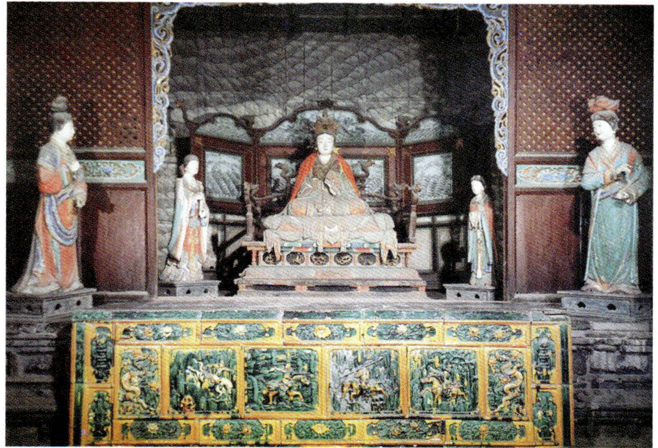

Sitting Saintly Mother and her maids, Hall of Saintly Mother of Jinci Memorial Temple, Northern Song.

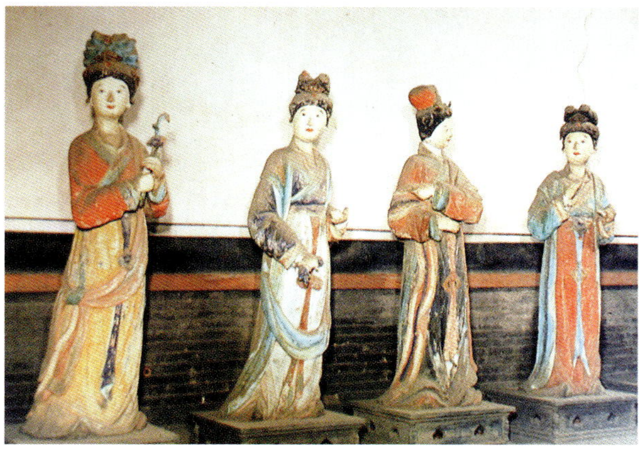

Statues of maids, Hall of Saintly Mother of Jinci Memorial Temple, Northern Song.

buildings. There are forty-three colored sculptures in the Goddess Hall. The main statue sits straight in the wood niche with four maids and two female officials in front of her standing in a fan shape. Eighteen attendants stand in a U-shape along the main niche. Although there are many statues the area is not cluttered.

The Goddess is dressed in a chaplet and official robes decorated with flowers and birds. It is highly decorous in appearance. The

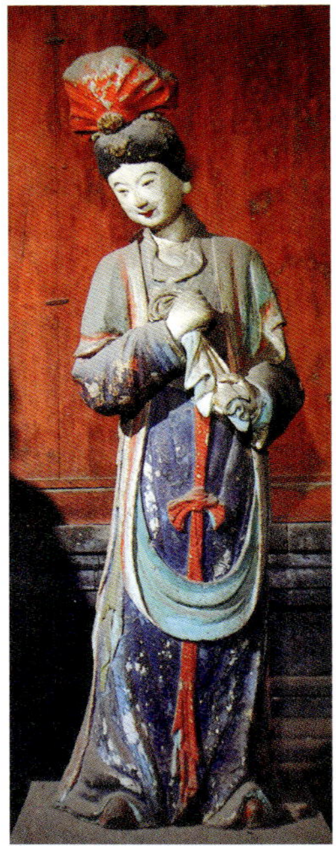
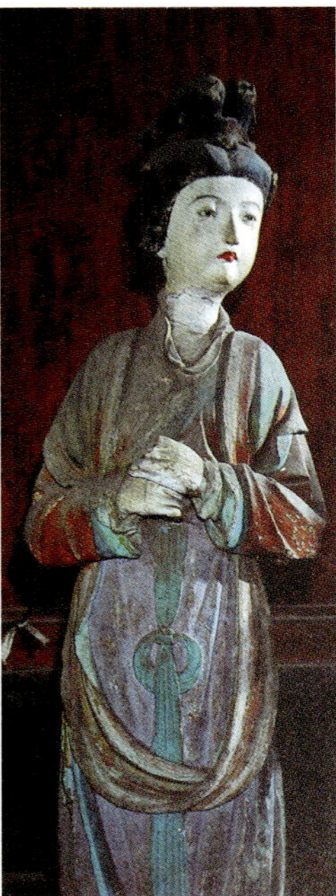
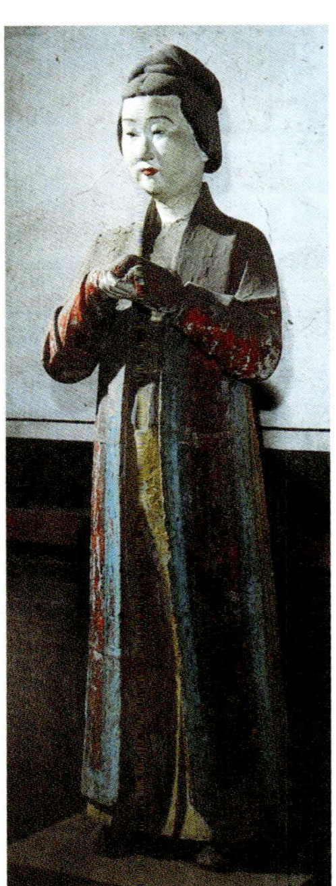

Three standing maids, Hall of Saintly Mother of Jinci Memorial Temple, Northern Song.

robe appears to have a soft and delicate quality and matches her body structure. In the image of the Goddess, the influence of Buddhism is visible. The Goddess is placed on the chancel of the main hall. She sits with her legs crossed. However, the hands of the Goddess are not exposed but hidden in her sleeves, suggesting an introverted temperament.

Buddhist Statues at Qinglian Temple

The Qinglian Temple is on the side of Xiashi Mountain in Zezhou County, Jincheng, Shanxi Province. There is a statue of Sakyamuni on the lotus throne in this temple, which gives it its name. It consists of two parts: An old and a new temple, which are conveniently nestled against the mountain. The elegant and neat buildings and courtyards are located amid the beautiful mountains and clear waters.

The old temple was built during the Northern Qi Dynasty (550–577). It includes a main hall and southern hall. A giant statue of Sakyamuni with two disciples on each side is located in the middle of the main hall. Two statues of Bodhisattvas, Manjusri Bodhisattva and Samantabhadra Bodhisattva sit opposite each other in front of the giant statues. The statues in the old temple were made during the Song Dynasty. The gold-overlaid statue of Sakyamuni is majestic with ears hanging low. The statue is wearing a loose Buddhist robe with a naked right shoulder. The statue sits on the lotus throne with the left hand on its knee and the right hand up in the air as if imparting Buddhist doctrines. The statues of Manjusri Bodhisattva and Samantabhadra Bodhisattva are mild in appearance with knots of hair on their heads. They are in brilliant clothes and wear necklaces and bracelets. The Manjusri Bodhisattva raises his hands in front of chest, while the Samantabhadra Bodhisattva puts the left hand on his knee and raises his right hand up. The southern hall contains many Tang-style Buddhist statues in the images of Sakyamuni, Manjusri, Samantabhadra, Kashyapa, Anada and other Bodhisattvas.

The new temple was built during the Sui Dynasty (581–618). The sculptures of the Song Dynasty are mostly in the Sakyamuni Hall and the auxiliary halls on both sides. The statues of Sakyamuni, Manjusri Bodhisattva and Samantabhadra Bodhisattva are in the Sakyamuni Hall. The statue of Sakyamuni has a wide face, golden hair and majestic appearance. His ears hang low and the right forearm has been damaged. The statues of Manjusri Bodhisattva and Samantabhadra Bodhisattva have a similar appearance with knot of hair, red crown, round face and long eyebrows. Their eyes are soft as if they are looking down at the world. They are wearing similar necklaces and similar clothes with different patterns. They are also very similar in appearance. Due to the ravages of time, their hands are damaged.

The auxiliary halls on both sides include statues of Manjusri Bodhisattva, sixteen Arhats, Ksitigarbha and Yamarajas. All these statues were made during the Song Dynasty. Among the majestic and vivid statues, those of Yamarajas are most distinctive. Yamarajas are ten unique images of Buddhist sculptures from China.

According to Indian Buddhism, there is only one Yamaraja to lead the deities of hell, judge dead people on their living deeds and hand out proper punishment. As Buddhism spread in China, some Buddhist deities were adopted by the Chinese and images of Yamarajas with distinctive Chinese features emerged as Buddhism met the needs of the Chinese people. These Yamarajas have a Chinese family name and there are definite records of their horoscopes. They are the continuous images of human rulers and the ruling class in hell. The sculptures of the Yamarajas in the new temple wear crowns and long beards. Some scowl at people, some are in the image of gentle officials, some are like wise old men. These images are similar to the images of deities from Taoism and far from their origin as images of Indian Buddhism.

Dazu rock carvings

Dazu rock carvings are an exceptional series of rock carvings in the Moya Grottoes, Dazu County, Sichuan Province. The carvings date to the Tang Dynasty (650) and were built over 1,200 years. The period from the Year of Yuanfeng in the Northern Song Dynasty to the Year of Chunyou in the Southern Song Dynasty (1078–1252) was the golden age of the Dazu rock carvings. The carvings made during the Song Dynasty are the essence of these carvings.

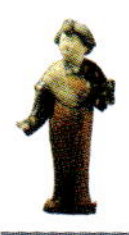

The carvings are mostly on the North Mountain, Baoding Mountain, South Mountain, Shizhuan Mountain and Shimen Mountain. The carvings of Esoteric Buddhism are gathered on South Mountain and Baoding Mountain, carvings of Taoism on South Mountain, carvings of Buddhism, Taoism and Confucianism on Shizhuan Mountain, and carvings of Taoism and Buddhism on Mountain. The Buddhist doctrines are popularly demonstrated by means of serial pictures there, combining the Buddha dharma, filial duty and filial rule from Confucian thought and pastoral feeling from Taoism. There, Buddhist doctrines further integrate with Chinese features. Popular thoughts and folk expressions are a major characteristic of Dazu rock carvings.

Shizhuan Mountain

The Moya Carving on Shizhuan Mountain began during the first century AD. It harmoniously combines Buddhism, Taoism and Confucianism, a rare combination among Chinese grottoes.

The No.6 Grotto is a shrine built for Confucius and his ten disciples. Confucius sits properly with a serious countenance in the middle of the shrine with his feet on a square table. He wears a headband and *hanfu* (the national costume of Han people) with a jade belt at the waist and a precious fan in his right hand. His ten disciples are in orderly rows on both sides of the Master, five on each side. They are vivid in appearance. Some face the Master, some stand with eyes to the front, while some are

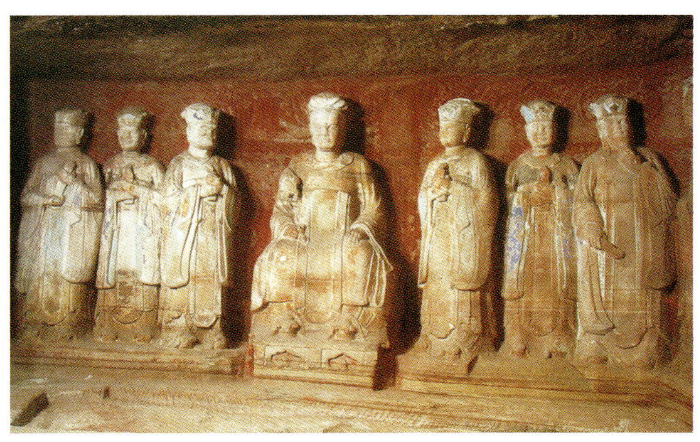

Confucius and his ten disciples, Dazu Rock Carvings, Northern Song.

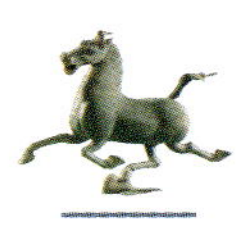

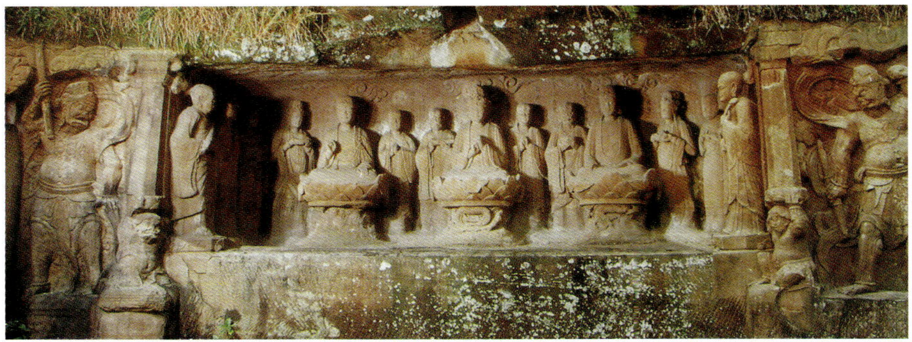

Three incarnations of Dharma-kaya, Dazu Rock Carvings, Northern Song.

in discussion with nearby disciples. They wear crowns and *hanfu* with jade belts and jade tablets in their hands. The carvings of Confucius and his ten disciples are clearly an imitation of the emperor and his officials.

The No.7 Grotto contains various carvings in the image of Buddha, Buddhists and Bodhisattva.

The No.8 Grotto is a shrine to Laozi. In the center of the shrine sits a statue of Laozi with seven statues of Taoist holy men standing on each sides. Laozi sits with his legs tucked up on a high table. The statue of Laozi is higher than the others. He is wearing a *hanfu* and has a fan in one hand. Other statues hold jade tablets. No.8 Grotto is similar to No.6.

Shimen Mountain

The carvings of Shimen Mountain were made between 1094 and 1151 and consist of twelve grottoes. The carvings present the harmonious combination of Buddhism and Taoism. The Taoist statues are most distinctive.

The No.2 Grotto was built during the Song Dynasty (1147) and is a shrine to the Jade Emperor. The statue of the Jade Emperor is small and sits on a throne in a dignified position. He wears a crown and imperial gowns and holds a jade tablet for ritual

Water-Moon Guanyin
It is said in Buddhist scripture that Buddha Guanyin had thirty-three dharma bodies with different appearances. The water-moon Guanyin refers to one watching the moon's shadow in water. There are many appearances, with a common sculpture being Guanyin standing amid lotus pedals, watching the moon's shadow in the water, and another is Guanyin sitting with crossed legs like lotus pedals on a rock in the sea. In addition, there are sitting Guanyin sculptures and sculptures with three faces and six arms. The image of water-moon Guanyin, one of the most frequently portrayed images in China's Buddhist sculpture, was found in Qianfodong, Dunhuang.

services in one hand with two maids holding large fans behind him. Two rare statues of a clairvoyant and a clairaudient are carved under the shrine. The clairvoyant's hair is put up with a hair decoration. He is wearing breast armor with a magic weapon in his right hand. He has a thin face with a pair of dilated eyes and an open mouth. The shape of the statue looks as if he is investigating a situation far away. The statue of the clairaudient is very ugly. His face is scrunched and exaggerated. A pair of erected ears looks as if he is listening. He is stripped to the waist and holds a snake-shaped magic weapon with one end in his hand and the other end around his neck. The two deities stand barefoot with two legs stretched out. The sculptural style gives them a kind of unstoppable power.

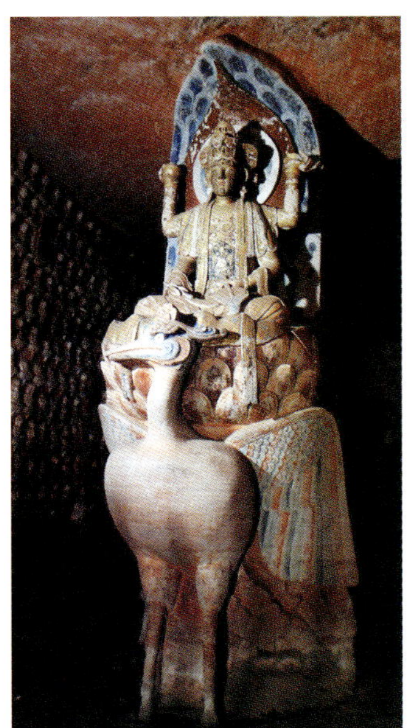
Grotto of Sutra of the Peahen Queen, Dazu Rock Carvings, Southern Song.

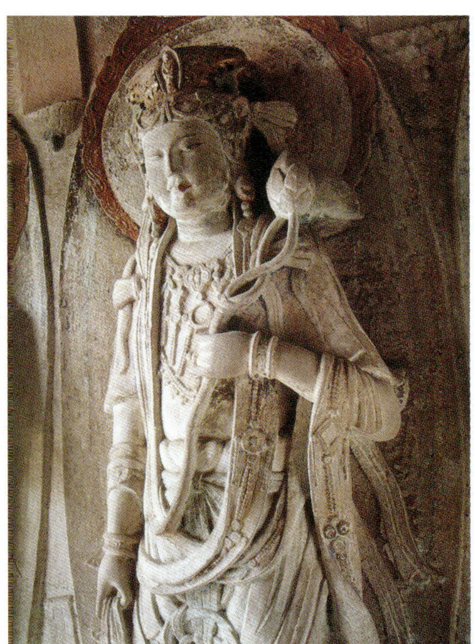
Bodhisattvas in Ten Saint Guanyin Grottoes, Dazu Rock Carvings, Southern Song.

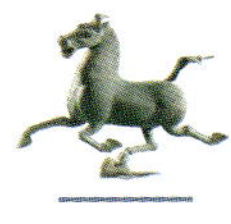

The Buddhist carvings are the shrines of Medicine Buddha, Guanyin and Sakyamuni, and grottoes of Guanyin and other Bodhisattvas. The No.6 Grotto of Guanyin is most exquisite. The grotto was built during the Song Dynasty (1141). In the center of the grotto is the statue of Amitabha with Guanyin and Mahasthamaprapta on the left and right sides respectively. They have elegant faces with wreathes on their heads, necklaces around the neck and soft Buddhist robes. The statue of Guanyin holds a lotus in front, while Mahasthamaprapta holds a *ruyi* (an auspicious object usually made of jade). On the left and right walls of the grotto is the statue of holy Guanyin with rounded face, peaceful appearance, slender figure, beautiful jewelry and ribbons around the body. The statue stands on twin lotus with bare feet. The divine light around the statue fully displays its elegance and charm. It is a masterpiece of grotto carving from the Song Dynasty.

Besides the abovementioned Jinci Temple, Qinglian Temple and Dazu rock carvings, the harmonious combination of Buddhism, Taoism and Confucianism are a common scene in temples built during the Song Dynasty, including the Prajna Cave in the Anyue Grottoes of the Southern Song Dynasty, the Lotus Temple (*Lianhua Ci*) Grottoes in Pingdingchuan, Gansu Province, and the holy shrine of the Northern Song Dynasty. These examples illustrate the change of Chinese religion. On the one hand, Buddhist thoughts gradually integrated with traditional Confucian culture and become part of the Chinese culture. On the other, the speculative philosophy of Buddhism promoted the growth of Confucianism during the Song Dynasty, while Taoism also adopted and borrowed ideas from Buddhism and Confucianism. Song-style sculptural arts combining Buddhism, Taoism and Confucianism directly reflect such intrinsic changes among the religious spirits.

Colorful Sculptures from the Ming and Qing Dynasties

Painted Sculptures from Temples

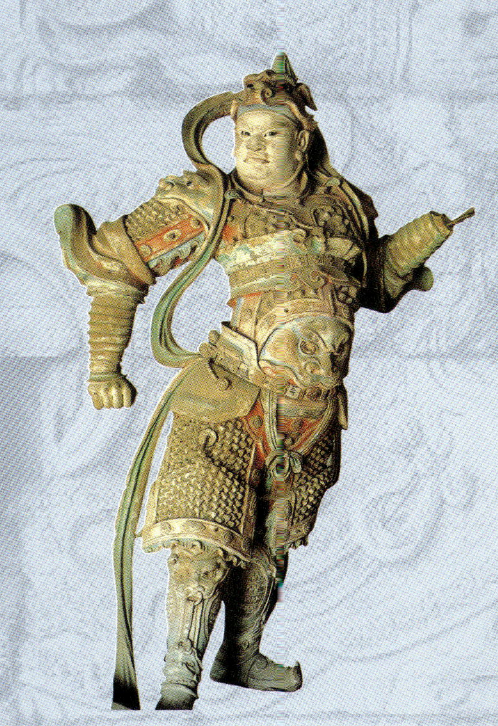

Although sculptures made during the Ming and Qing dynasties followed traditions from previous dynasties, most are less majestic and powerful than those of the Han and Tang dynasties. Sculptural arts are often connected with the spiritual state of people and social conditions. Changes mainly lie in the decline of religious thinking and the rise of traditional aesthetic consciousness. As the urban economy grew, grotto carvings were replaced by temple arts. As a result, there are almost no grotto carvings from this period.

Though there are many masterpieces among the temple sculptures, most are highly stylized and lack vitality. Traditional images of deities such as Guan Yu, local god of the land and town, became popular. Religious sculptures became mediocre and less creative due to lack of religious belief. But architecture related to Buddhism, Taoism and Confucianism continued to grow quickly and worship of various and complicated idols emerged. Generally speaking, Ming and Qing-style religious sculptures tended to be stylized while folk sculptures are more ornamental.

Buddhism and Taoism also became more popular during this period, supported by the ruling class. The golden age of Buddhism had past. The Qing Dynasty even issued rules to standardize Buddhist sculptures. Under these rules, sculptures gradually became stylized and rigid. The sculptural arts declined dramatically.

Yet despite changes in the nature of religion, the number of temple sculptures continued to grow. Ming-style sculptures are mostly painted sculptures based on clay bodies, while Qing-style sculptures widely adopted bronze and wood bodies. Sculptures made during this period followed the Tang and Song-style in shape and style but also reflected the distinctive features of their time.

Sculptures from this period are more realistic, exquisite and ornamental. They are closely associated with the growth of technological skills. The most significant Ming-style clay sculptures are kept in the Shuanglin Temple in Pingyao, Shanxi Province. Qing-style painted sculptures are found in Qiongzhu Temple in Kunming, Yunnan Province.

Ming-style painted sculptures at Shuanglin Temple

Shuanglin Temple was built during the Northern Wei Dynasty. Formerly called Zhongdu Temple, its name was changed after the Song Dynasty, according to Buddhist scriptures. It was well known even during the Song Dynasty because of the old, well-preserved stone tablet inscriptions in this temple. The existing buildings were mainly rebuilt during the Ming and Qing dynasties. A large number of painted sculptures are well preserved — 1,566 out of 2,052 pieces in the temple. They are mainly full relief, high relief and low relief pieces as well as unique suspending sculptures and sculptures hanging on walls. They

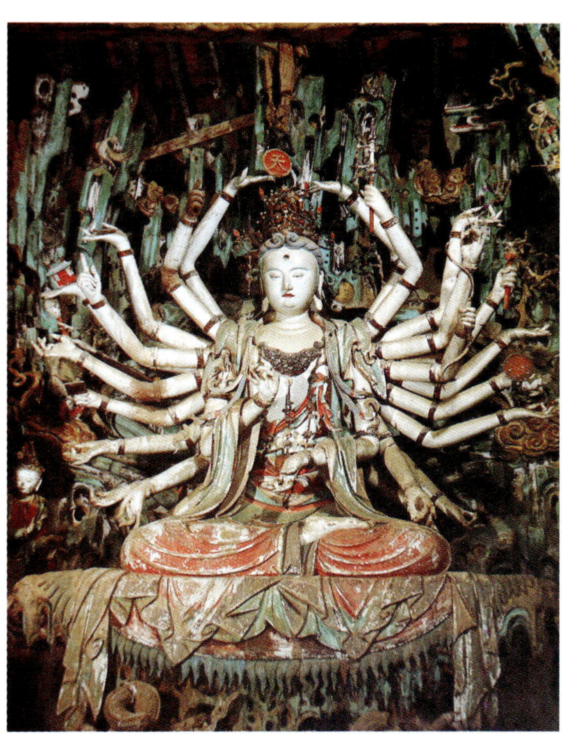

Statue of the Thousand-Hand Bodhisattva, Shuanglin Temple, Pingyao, Shanxi, Ming Dynasty.

are the masterpieces of the master-hands and a valuable cultural heritage. Therefore, Shuanglin Temple in Pingyao is also called a "Treasure House of Oriental Painted Sculptures" and a "Museum of Painted Sculpture."

Statues of Four Heavenly Guardians

The painted sculptures in the Shuanglin Temple are creative and vivid. They possess distinctive Buddhist characteristics. For example, the statues of the Four Heavenly Guardians in Shuanglin Temple stand in a line side by side. They are unique not only in their size and arrangement but also style and shape. They fully reflect the unique talent of their creators. Many statues of the same kind made during the Ming Dynasty only pay attention to unusual images rather than to personality and temperament. The statues in the Shuanglin Temple borrow ideas from the images of warriors, which give them gigantic force, heroic appearance and strong vitality.

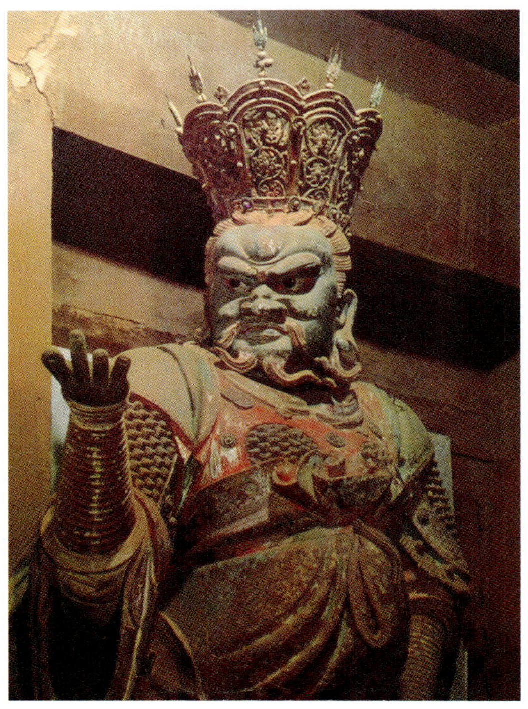

Dhanada, Shuanglin Temple, Pingyao, Shanxi, Ming Dynasty.

Statues of Eighteen Arhats

Besides the statues of the Four Heavenly Guardians, there are many other breathtaking painted sculptures, such as the statues of *arhats*, *guanyin* and other idols, in the temple.

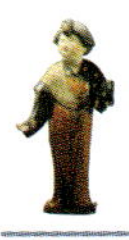

The Hall of Four Heavenly Guardians is the first courtyard, including the main hall (Hall of Sakyamuni) and auxiliary halls (Hall of Arhats, Hall of Guangong, Hall of Yamaraja and Hall of God of Land). But it is the Hall of Arhats that is the essence of the temple. The statues of Eighteen Arhats are masterpieces. These life-size statues are in proper proportion and structure. They are honored as "holy works." According to Chinese Buddhism, the arhats have the nature of Buddha and are similar to Buddhists on earth. Therefore, the statues of *arhats* can easily break the restraints of religion and possess the personality of man. The statues in the Hall of Arhats have steady personalities and vivid shapes. They are soft on the outside and hard inside.

The Statue of Dumb Arhat is most remarkable. He wears a cowl and sits cross-legged in the hall. His body is symmetrical. His posture is erect and his robe covers his hands. This statue produces a feeling of infinite thinking and power. His facial expression is most distinctive. His eyes reveal his anger. His integrity and understanding eyes make a deep impression. In fact, most painted sculptures from Shuanglin Temple have vivid eyes. Sculptors from the Ming Dynasty attached great importance to the eyes of the statues, where are anatomically correct. The structures of eyebrows, eye sockets and eyeballs on the statues are similar to the structure of the human body. In order to express the vivid eyes, the sculptors used black lazurite or black paint to make the eyeballs, which adds the finishing touch to the statues.

Statue of Zizai Guanyin

The Grand Hall, the Thousand-Buddha Hall and the Bodhisattva Hall are located in the second courtyard. The statues in the Thousand-Buddha Hall are of great significance in this temple. The significance lies in a statue of Zizai Guanyin and a statue of Veda. The Shuanglin Temple includes a large number of statues of *guanyin*, including Duhai Guanyin and

Thousand-Hand Guanyin, which are usually sitting in a posture of "mind in comfort and ease." The statue of Zizai Guanyin does not follow the traditional standing posture but sits at ease. The statue has its right leg lifted and the right arm on the right knee. It is unique in the history of the Chinese sculpting.

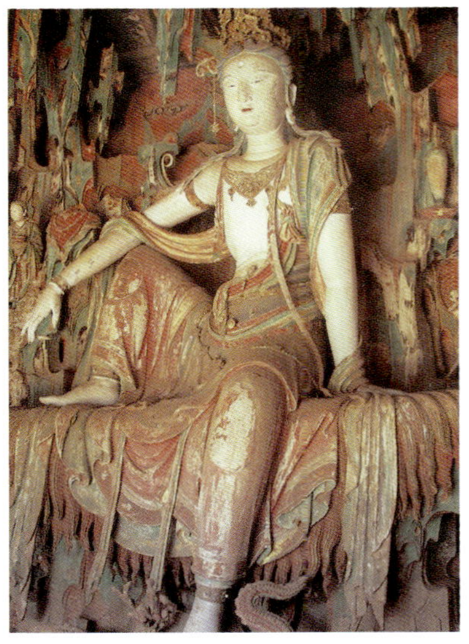

Statue of Guanyin Bodhisattva, Shuanglin Temple, Pingyao, Shanxi, Ming Dynasty.

Statue of Veda

The Statue of Veda in an aggressive posture is also a brilliant example from the Shuanglin Temple. Veda is the Guardian Deity in Buddhism. The statue in Shuanglin Temple has both civil character and military competence. It looks powerful and fierce. The statue has an exaggerated body and vivid facial expression, especially the eyes, which appear to follow you from all sides.

The sculptors used this static statue to display dynamic charm, an important reason why this statue meets with great artistic success. The weight of the statue is on its right foot. Its two legs are in front and the upper body is distorted to the right from the head to the waist. The distortion greatly exceeds the physical limits of the human body. However, the posture does not produce an uncomfortable feeling but gives it great power. It looks like an S-shaped curve, which gives the statue more vitality and a dynamic feeling. The statue also displays a sense of rhythm and continuity of movement.

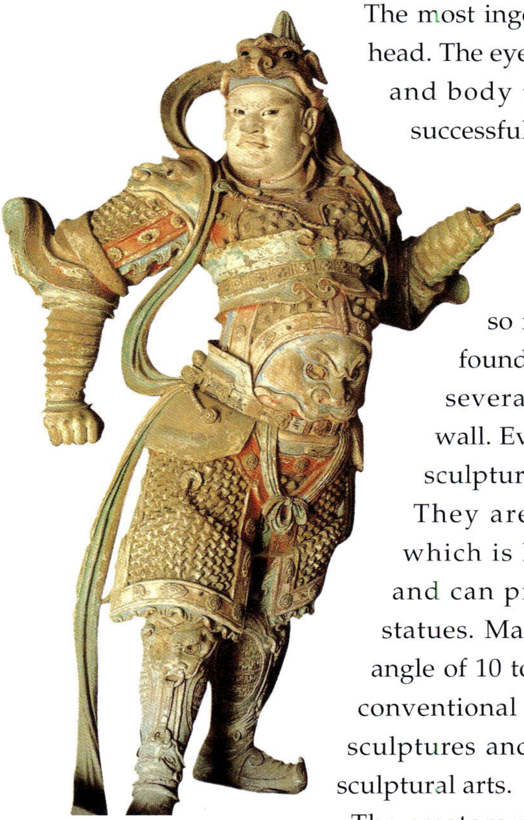

The most ingenious designs are the eyes and head. The eyes look to the left, while the head and body turns to the right. The statue successfully breaks stylized restrains.

Characteristics and processing techniques

It is somewhat amazing that so many painted sculptures can be found in Shuanglin Temple. There are several hundred statues on just one wall. Every statue is perfect, not only in sculptural form but also in decoration. They are made of the local red clay, which is high in viscosity and quality and can produce smooth and exquisite statues. Many statues bend forward at an angle of 10 to 20 degrees, which changes the conventional processing method of the clay sculptures and combines mechanics and the sculptural arts.

Standing statute of Veda, Shuanglin Temple, Pingyao, Shanxi, Ming Dynasty.

The creators paid profound attention to the eyes. The eyeballs of most statues use black lazurite and are bright and piercing even after a thousand years. There are more than 2,000 painted sculptures, big and small, in Shuanglin Temple, all different in appearance and shape.

The painted sculptures in Shuanglin Temple follow the conventional method of Chinese clay sculptures. The method can be roughly divided in four steps.

The first step is to make a wooden frame, depending on the size of the statue. The frame, just like the human skeleton, plays a supportive role. The wooden frame was usually bound with straw and hemp rope to protect the clay from cracks and shrinking.

The second step was to add coarse clay. The coarse clay was added to the wooden frame in two or three steps. The clay was then closely compacted to the frame. Sand was mixed into the clay to protect the statue from cracking.

The third step was to add fine clay. The facial expressions, movements, cloth patterns, ribbons, necklaces and temperament of the statue were all completed in this step.

The fourth and final step was painting. After the clay body was completely dry, it was painted with two or three layers of gum. A couple of coats of powder mixed with egg were then applied. The egg white can give the statue luster and strength. After that, the statue was wiped repeatedly until the surface became smooth to complete the color painting. The paints used were mostly mineral paints, so the colors are still bright and fresh after several thousands of years.

Statues of Five Hundred *arhats* at Qiongzhu Temple

The statues of five hundred *arhats* in Qiongzhu Temple were made during the Guangxu Reign of the Qing Dynasty (c. 1883). They are all painted sculptures of around 1m in height. The statues are the most creative of all Buddhist sculptures from the Qing Dynasty. They are unique in their painted sculptural techniques and strong folk style.

These statues were made by Li Guangxiu, from Sichuan Province, a famous folk artist of the period. He was not only good at sculpting and painting but was also interested in Buddhism. It took Li Guangxiu and his apprentices more than twenty years to complete the statues. The statues are different in shape and

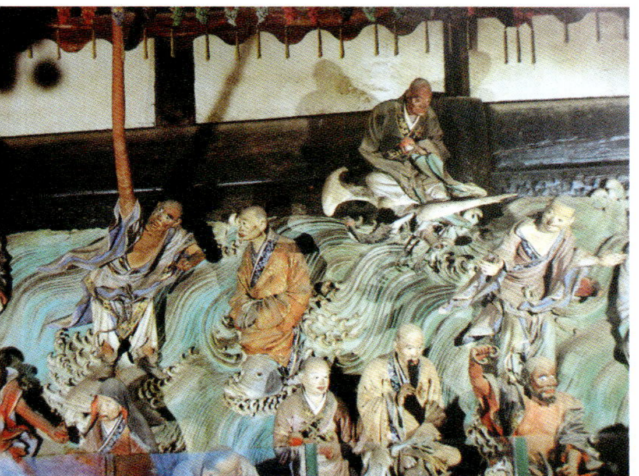

Group statues of five hundred *arhats* (south wall), Qiongzhu Temple, Kunming, Yunnan, Qing Dynasty.

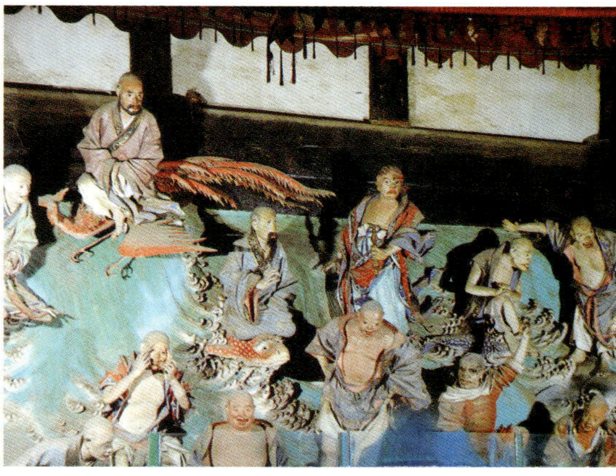

Group statues of five hundred *arhats* (north wall), Qiongzhu Temple, Kunming, Yunnan, Qing Dynasty.

each has its own character. Their clothes and properties are also various. No two statues are quite the same. The space between the statues varies but they are in their proper arrangement. Their hair and beards are all made of real hair. Their eyeballs are made of black lazurite. The statues are wearing folk style clothes and represent people from all walks of life, such as squires, scholars, merchants and butchers. Such strong secular styles are one of the characteristics of Qing-style Buddhist sculptures. These statues are famous for their realism.

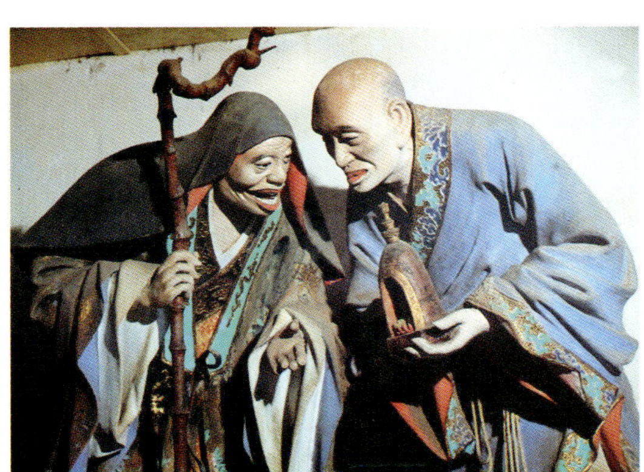

Group statues of *arhats* with wands, Qiongzhu Temple, Kunming, Yunnan, Qing Dynasty.

The statues borrow stage skills and features from the Chinese opera, especially Sichuan opera. They are endowed with vivid characteristics of worldly people. These statues could only be made in Yunnan,

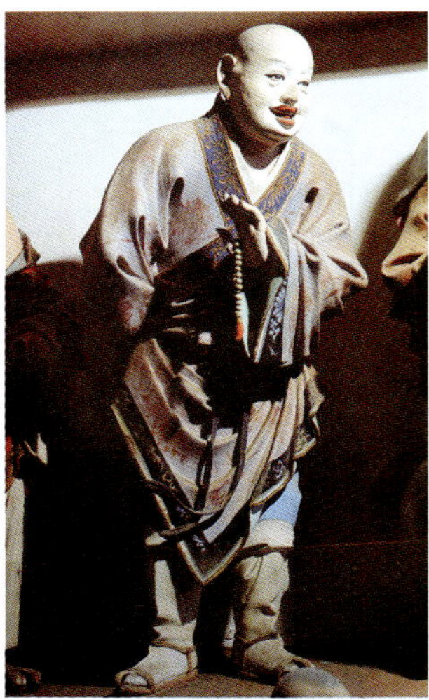

Arhats praying to Buddha, Qiongzhu Temple, Kunming, Yunnan, Qing Dynasty.

where religious ideas remained free during the late Qing Dynasty and the social environment was complicated.

Although there are some breathtaking masterpieces from the Ming and Qing dynasties, sculpture fell into decay during this period. The secular styles and developed techniques made sculptures from the Ming and Qing dynasties more luxurious but also sometimes gaudy and superficial.

"Separate Strokes, Connected Meaning"

"Separate strokes, connected meaning" means that the meaning of writing is still connected when the stroke breaks in drawing a Chinese painting or writing brush characters. The key is that the ending of each stroke prepares the beginning of another.

Beautiful Residences

Architectural Sculpting

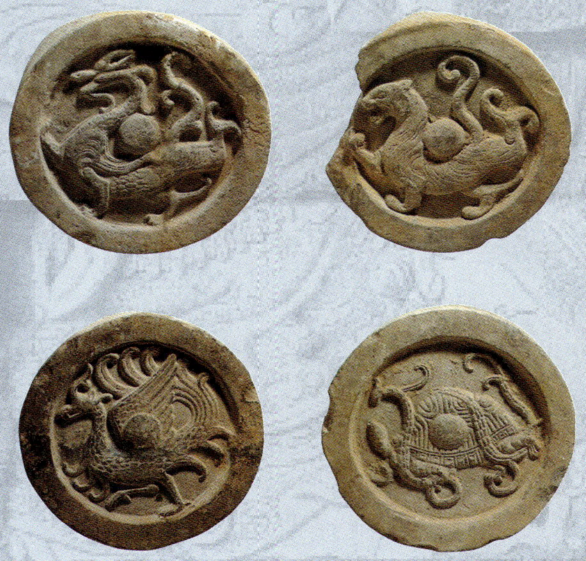

Classical Chinese architecture demonstrates not only concepts of traditional inhabitation but also the personal aesthetics of the Chinese people. It integrates ethics, social structure and world outlook. Chinese people thought architecture was similar to other technique-based craftwork. In other words, architecture was less elegant and significant than mainstream arts. However, the charm of classical Chinese architecture is still overwhelming. It does not rest on a single piece but in the harmonious integration of parts and a unique view of spatial layout. Ornamental sculptures used in architecture play an important role in contrasting the charm of architecture.

Classical Chinese architecture was based on wooden frames. Skillful frame structures fully display the wisdom of Chinese craftsmen and the scientific concept behind Chinese aesthetics. Palaces built for emperors of different periods are symbolic masterpieces of different periods. They reflect Chinese architectural ideas and philosophy along with changes of social customs and culture.

Qin tile carvings and Han tile ornaments

Since the early Qin Dynasty, brick carvings and eaves-tile ornaments have been popular. During the Spring and Autumn and the Warring States periods, each vassal state had its own characteristics for palace buildings. After Emperor Shihuang of the Qin Dynasty unified China, those characteristics carried into the Qin Dynasty and continued to evolve. Most of the architectural heritage of the Qin Dynasty uses half-round and round eaves-tile ornaments with distinctive ornamental purposes.

The eaves-tile ornament is also called eave-end, which is the overhang on eaves. It is mainly used to waterproof and

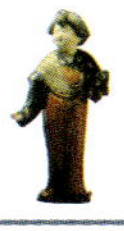

for drainage, to protect the wooden frame of a roof, as well as for ornamental purposes. During the Warring States Period, most eaves-tile ornaments of the State of Yan were carved with patterns of twin birds or beasts, while those of the State of Qi were carved with patterns of trees and clouds. Some round eaves-tile ornaments of the State of Qin and the State of Zhao were designed with patterns of birds or beasts.

It is said that the State of Qin built the spectacular Epang Palace after it unified China. Although this palace no longer exists, people can still imagine its magnificence through the site of another ancient palace, the second largest of the Qin Dynasty in Xianyan, Gansu Province. Large numbers of eaves-tile ornaments have been unearthed in Xianyan. They give some clues to Qin architectural style. The Qin Dynasty was more advanced than the Warring States Period in palace building. The Qin's eaves-tile ornaments are more exquisite and artistic. They include two designs: Characters and patterns. The patterns include clouds and animals. Such designs demonstrate the simple and concise features of Qin sculptural arts, which are different from the round and mature style of the Han Dynasty.

Many hollow tiles have been unearthed in Xianyan, Shanxi Province. Some are designed with dragon and phoenix relief sculptures, others use line-cutting techniques to display hunting images. The tiles fully demonstrate the level of sculpture and power during the Qin. Therefore, the Qin and Han dynasties are famous for tile carvings and eaves-tile ornaments respectively.

During the Western Han Period, as the architectural techniques used in palaces, temples and tombs evolved, tiles carvings and eaves-tile ornaments became popular. Round eaves-tile ornaments entered the mainstream. Character carvings on eaves-tile ornaments became popular during

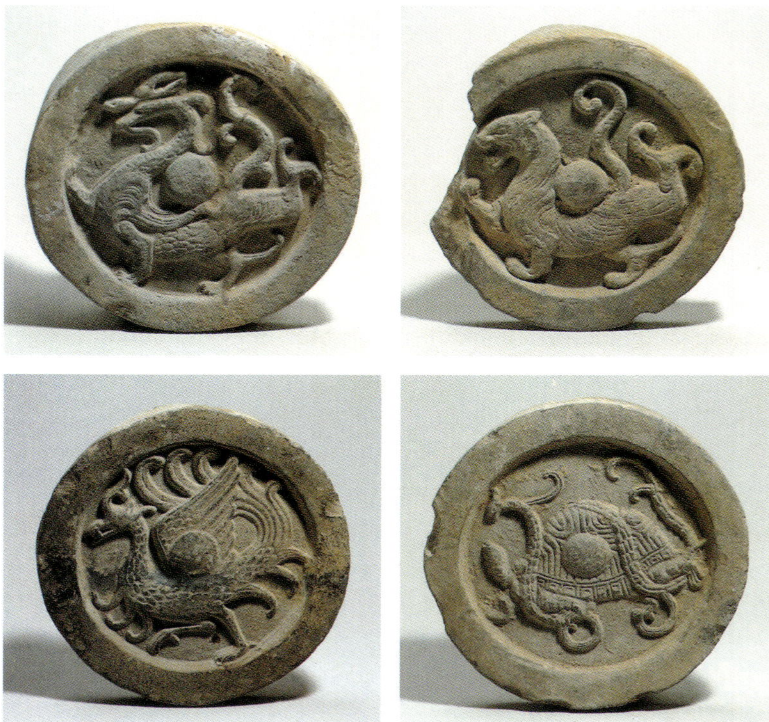

Round eaves-tile ornaments with four-deity pattern, Han Dynasty.

this period, reflecting splendid achievements in calligraphy and literature. Eaves-tile ornaments were endowed with special meaning. Various characters and patterns indicated symbolic meanings. Palace buildings used mostly round eaves-tile ornaments carved with four auspicious characters in seal or square styles, such as "长乐未央," "长生无极" or "延年益寿" (representing "longevity"). Some were carved with two auspicious characters, such as "万岁" and "无极," or messages with three, eight, or even nine auspicious characters. All these characters express wishes of longevity or happiness.

Besides characters, there were also animal patterns and combinations of characters and patterns. Among animal patterns, the most typical during the Han Dynasty was the pattern of "four divine animals," including *Qinglong* (green dragon), *Baihu* (white tiger), *Zhuque* (red phoenix) and *Xuanwu* (black turtle). These are symbols used to exorcise evil spirits and bring in auspiciousness. They represent the four directions (east, west, south and north) and the four seasons (spring, summer, autumn and winter). Each divine animal is carved in a circular shape without any constraint of feeling. The powerful and smooth carvings are brilliant masterpieces of ancient patterns.

Relief sculptures on *que* from the Eastern Han Dynasty

A *que*, similar to a tower, is a unique form of ancient Chinese architecture that includes a passage in the middle. It was usually built on both sides of a palace or tomb for decoration and as a safeguard. Early *que*-towers use stone and wood structures. Most currently preserved *que*-towers are stone ones.

These ornamental structures were very popular during the Eastern Han Dynasty. *Que*-towers in front of tombs were common, while those in front of temples were rare. Preserved *que*-towers from the Eastern Han Dynasty can be found mainly in Sichuan, then Henan and Shandong provinces. However, the *que*-towers in Sichuan stand out for their exquisite sculptural techniques. Each corner of the tower eaves includes relief sculptures. For example, *que*-towers in front of the tomb of the Master of Pingyangfu include two fighting tigers on each corner of tower eaves. Some *que*-towers in front of tombs have relief sculptures in the images of four divine animals and demonstrate typical Han styles.

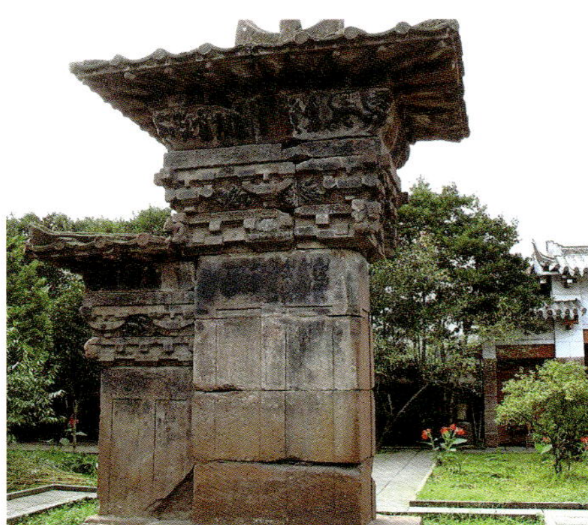

Stone statues in front of the tombs of Gao Yi, prefect of Yizhou, Sichuan and his younger brother Gao Shi, Eastern Han.

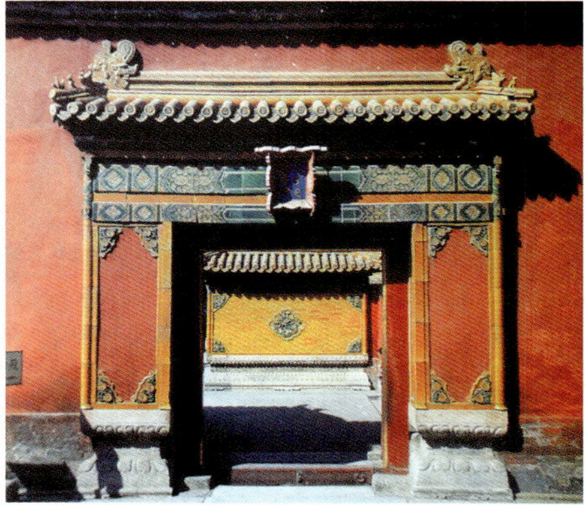

Screen wall inside Zunyi Gate in the Forbidden City, Qing Dynasty.

There are thirty-five unearthed stone *que*-towers from the Han Dynasty, including five with verified histories. The *que*-towers are surface structures. After several thousand years, most are damaged and their sculptures damaged. Therefore, the towers are more meaningful for their historical than their aesthetic value. However, the general look of Han's memorial sculptures can still be seen from existing sculptures on stone *que*-towers. Generally speaking, the stone *que*-tower of the Han Dynasty is unique in traditional Chinese architecture. After the Han Dynasty, various sculptures and murals on *que*-towers were still commonly seen. Over time, the *que*-tower developed into the *paifang* (memorial arch) and screen wall. During the Ming and Qing dynasties, the *que*-tower evolved into a kind of structure similar to the *wumen* of the Imperial Palace.

Ornamental architectural sculptures of the Sui and Tang Dynasties

During the Sui and Tang dynasties, ornamental sculptures were widely used due to the development of palace buildings and tombstones. According to historical materials, some imperial palaces including the Daxing Palace of the Sui Dynasty, and the Taiji Palace, Daming Palace and Xingqing Palace of the Tang Dynasty are exquisite and gorgeous. Compared to the Qin and Han dynasties, the Sui and Tang dynasties produced more splendid ornamental sculptures but threw a shade on the artistic value of tile patterns. Most palace buildings during the Tang Dynasty are made of brick with patterns in the shapes of lotus and grapes.

The lotus-shaped pattern is closely associated with the spread of Buddhism during the Tang Dynasty, while grape-shaped patterns are connected to the cultural exchanges between the Central Plains and the Western Regions (*Xiyu*) in ancient times. Though elegant and splendid, Tang-style architectural sculptures are less dignified and powerful than Qin and Han-style sculptures, though they fully demonstrate the confidence and cultural tolerance of the Tang Dynasty. Eaves-tile ornaments are small and simple. These changes have an intimate relation with changes in ornamental focus. Painted lacquer and sunk-panels were also adopted by the Tang architects. More attention was transferred from eaves-tile ornaments to other parts of architecture.

However, there are no extant palace buildings from the Sui and Tang dynasties. The Sui and Tang-style architectural sculptures we see today are only from a limited number of Buddhist pagodas and bridges. We can only find clues to the appearance of palace buildings of this period from some architectural heritage and historical materials. For example, Anji Bridge, a bridge from the Sui Dynasty in Hebei Province, was made of stone with various ornamental sculptures. It fully displays the ornamental style of the dynasty. One railing panel on the bridge is designed with a *jiao* (scaly dragon)-shaped pattern, which follows the *kui*-shaped pattern on the bronze wares of the Shang Dynasty.

According to the *New History of the Tang Dynasty* and the *Old History of the Tang Dynasty*, there are records of Empress Wu Zetian building *Tianshu* (a kind of memorial column). In the late seventh century, Empress Wu Zetian built a memorial column over 30m high in the ancient city of Luoyang to symbolize her achievements in the establishment of the Dazhou Dynasty (690–705). This column was designed with exquisite patterns of dragons, *kylin* and phoenix. Although it no longer exists, we still can imagine its elegant look from other memorial columns from the Tang Dynasty.

The Big Wild Goose Pagoda in Xi'an is one of the most famous Buddhist pagodas in China. It was built in the early Tang Dynasty as a chamber for the translation of Buddhist scriptures for Master Xuanzang (Monk Tripitaka). Its door frames and lintels are carved with various ornamental paintings - mainly images of Buddhas, Bodhisattvas and Four Heavenly Guardians - by means of intaglio. Its ornamental styles and subjects are similar to works of the same kind in grottoes. It displays the features of *tiexianmiao*-style from ancient Chinese painting. The Dragon and Tiger Pagoda in Jinan, Shandong Province, is another Buddhist pagoda from the Tang Dynasty with brilliant ornamental sculptures. It is designed with patterns in the image of Buddha, Apsaras, lions and pictures of dance movements on its pedestal and Apsaras, Buddhas, dragons and Heavenly Guardians on the main body. The pattern is splendid in color and complete in structure.

Wooden architecture evolved further during the Song Dynasty. Many palace and temple buildings from the Song Dynasty adopted painted ornaments rather than sculptural ornaments due to the development of painting arts. Carved bricks were only seen in tombs.

Stone architectural sculptures of the Yuan Dynasty

During the Yuan Dynasty, architectural sculptures were rather advanced. According to the records, there were jade and stone mills to make architectural sculptures for the emperor. Though palace buildings of the Yuan Dynasty no longer exist, we know that palace buildings of the Ming and Qing dynasties

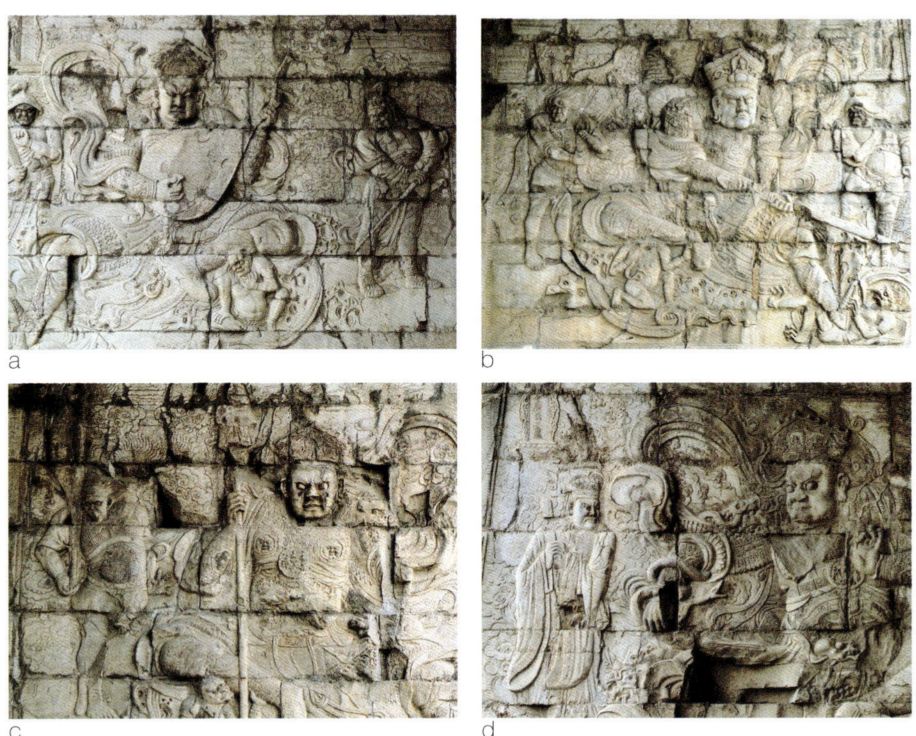

Relief of four deities inside the archway of the Clouds Terrace near the Juyongguan Pass, Yuan Dynasty.
a Dhrtarastra b Irudhaka c Dhanada d Virupaksa

followed the traditions and styles of the Yuan Dynasty in both ornamentation and sculpture.

The Clouds Terrace near the Juyongguan Pass in Changping District, Beijing, is the most important Yuan-style sculpture. The Clouds Terrace, the pedestal of the Over-Street Tower, was built in 1342 and is located on the road to the Capital of the Yuan Dynasty. The terrace is famous for its relief sculptures in the image of the Four Heavenly Guardians inside the arch and the ornamental sculptures outside the arch. They are brilliant masterpieces of architectural sculptures of the Yuan Dynasty. Relief sculptures of Four Heavenly Guardians have very exaggerated shapes to show their power. They vividly reflect the culture of the Yuan Dynasty, which was powerful but short of cultural cohesion.

Architectural Sculptures of the Ming and Qing Dynasties

Many buildings from the Ming and Qing dynasties have survived.

Architectural sculptures are also common. Besides imperial gardens, temples and tombs, folk architectural sculptures are also profound and centered on public buildings such as academies, ancestral temples and commercial chambers.

Nine-Dragon Patterns of Imperial Gardens

The Forbidden City is an outstanding representative of imperial architectural sculptures. It uses dragons and phoenixes as its major ornamental subjects and various sculptural techniques such as high and low-relief sculpting and openwork and circular carvings. It is more exquisite and splendid than those of the previous dynasties and perfectly combines the sculptures' ornamental and practical features. Though its sculptural

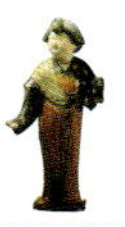

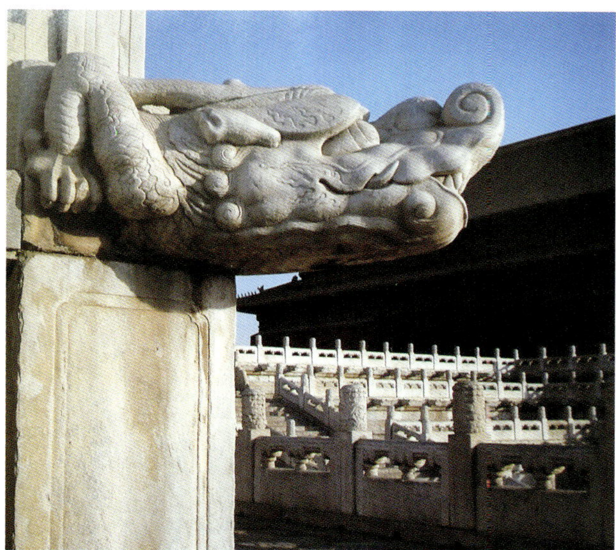

A discharge spout in the shape of the dragon's head at the pedestals of the three main halls of the Palace Museum, Ming and Qing dynasties.

ornaments look a little complicated, they perfectly represent imperial power.

The pedestals of the three main halls of the Forbidden City are enclosed with white marble carving railings and balusters. The top of the balusters is engraved with raised cloud-dragon and Phoenix patterns. The bottom of each baluster has a discharge spout made into the shape of the dragon's head - *Chi*. The *yudao* (road used only by the emperor) is carved out of three big rocks running through north-south to the steps of the three main halls. The *yudao* in the shape of nine dragons under the Hall of Preserving Harmony is the most representative road. It is carved out of a whole piece of stone that is 16m long and 3m wide and weighs more than 200 tons. The lower end of the *yudao* is engraved with symbolic patterns of five great mountains. The top is carved with nine huge dragons slipping through the clouds and seas. Every three dragons are lined up in the shape of the Chinese character "品", nine dragons are arranged in three groups from top to bottom, known as "nine dragons playing with pearls." The two sides of the *yudao* are engraved with tangled tree branch designs in low

Chi

Chi, also known as *Chi* Head, is one of the nine sons of the dragon in ancient folklore. Because it has a big mouth and its stomach can contain a lot of water, *Chi* was often used as the rainspout decoration in China's palace architecture. The earliest existing building relics are the stone *Chi* Head of the Northern and Southern dynasties. In the Song Dynasty, it became a practice to use the *Chi* Head in buildings.

relief, which were re-carved during the twenty-fifth year of the Qianlong period (1760).

The architectural sculpture that is based on the nine dragons also includes a nine-dragon screen. There are three excellent representatives of nine-dragon screens. The first is in Beihai Park; the second in Ningshou Palace (Palace of Peace and Longevity) of the Forbidden City and the third is in Datong, Shanxi Province. The nine-dragon screen is actually a screen wall engraving with the pattern of nine dragons. The screen wall is usually located in front of or inside the gate of a house to shelter it from view of the courtyard. Therefore, pedestrians cannot look into the courtyard and guests can tidy themselves in front of the screen wall before visiting the host. Screen walls in ancient China were arranged by grade. According to the ritual system of the Western Zhou, only palaces, accommodations of lords and temples could use screen walls. During the Ming and Qing dynasties, common people also set screen walls in their courtyards; the quadrangles in Beijing are a model.

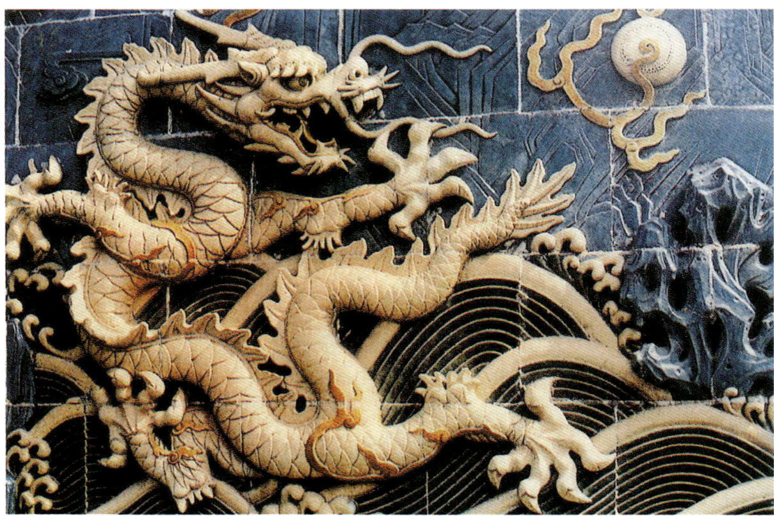

Nine-dragon screen (detail) at Beihai Park, Qing Dynasty.

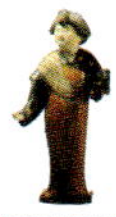

The nine-dragon screen in Beihai Park was built during the twenty-first year of Qianlong. The whole wall is 26m long, 7m high and nearly 1.5m thick. It is composed of 424 glazed tiles that emboss the screen. There are nine huge dragons on each side of the screen, with big or small dragons in different postures decorating the two ends and the eaves, making a surprising total of 635 dragons.

The nine-dragon screen in the Ningshou Palace was built in 1771 during the reign of Emperor Qianlong. Its pattern is similar to that of the Beihai Park, but the details are quite different.

The nine-dragon screen in Datong was built in 1392 for the thirteenth son of Zhu Yuanzhang, the first Emperor of the Ming Dynasty. It has been well preserved and remains intact to this day. It is nearly 43m long, 8m high and 2m thick. It is the largest of these works. The pedestal of a statue of Buddha on the screen wall is engraved with patterns of lions, tigers, elephants, *kylin* and horses. The top is a mill-framed structure. The most eye-catching part is the pool in front of the screen wall, in which the nine dragons are reflected. When the winds drift along the water surface, it looks as if the nine dragons are playing in the water, showing a vivid and artful design.

Lions

The lion has been the guardian of palaces and tombs since the Han Dynasty. It was developed into an image that is both like and unlike an actual lion during the later Qing period. In ancient China, the lion has always been considered as a precious and auspicious animal. After Buddhism was introduced into China, it was endowed with holiness.

Images of lions in the palaces of the Ming and Qing are stone carvings or bronze statues with square pedestals like those given to a statue of Buddha. Most lion statues squat at two sides of the gate. The gate is guarded on either side by a huge statue of a female and a male lion. The male lion steps on the *siukiu* while the female lion plays with a young lion.

Lion statues in the Palace Museum include two main types. One is the stone lions in front of Tian'anmen and the bronze lions in front of the Taihe (the Gate of Supreme Peace) Gate. They are powerful and martial, with the mighty character of the palaces. The second type is embodied by the gilt bronze lions in front of Qianqingmen (the Gate of Celestial Purity). By size, they are not as strong as the first type but they are more exquisite and complicated. These lions are exquisitely wrought and are similar in decoration to the *kylin* or other auspicious animals. In fact, the differences are based on the designers' consideration of the different functions of the palaces and outer courts. Tian'anmen and Taihe Gate are the places where emperors held ceremonies and made important decisions. These places show the awesome dignity of the palaces and royalty, so the lion statues have a strong sense of dignity. Qianqingmen and Ningshoumen were the private quarters where royals lived, so they did not

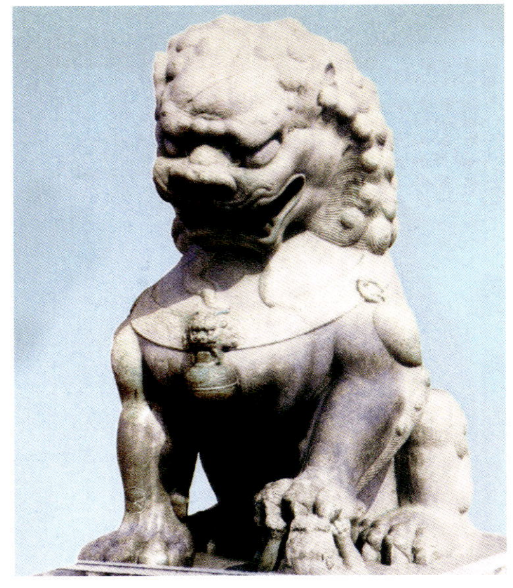

A stone lion in front of the Tian'anmen Rostrum of the Forbidden City, Ming and Qing dynasties.

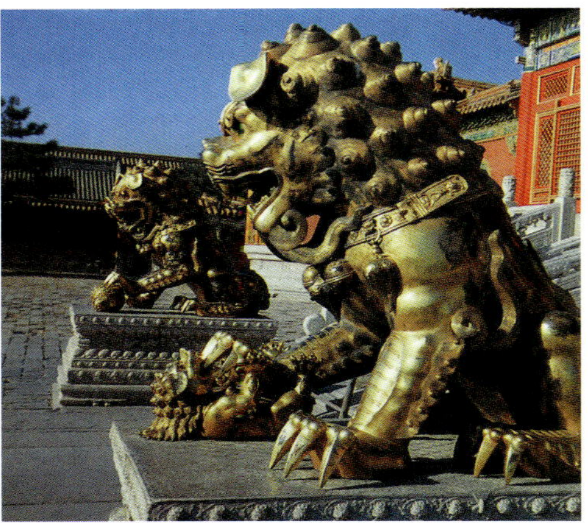

Gilt bronze lions in front of Ningshou Gate of the Forbidden City, Ming and Qing dynasties.

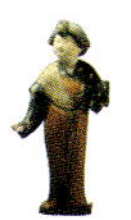

need a style full of dignity and strength, but are exquisite, kind and decorative.

Lion images were not thought to belong just to the royals. Small stone lions could be used to the protect houses of regular people. For instance, in the rural areas of northern Shaanxi Province, local people placed stone lions on the edge of their *kang* (brick beds) to exorcise evil spirits and protect children.

Folk architectural sculpture

Besides the architectural sculptures of palaces, there are also many folk architectural sculptures displaying diverse themes and excellent skill. Common architectural sculptures are brick sculptures and woodcarving. Some sculptures are affected by images of birds, flowers and figures showing scenes of birds and flowers and stories.

Folk sculptures form different regional styles. The woodcarving in Chaozhou of Guangdong Province and the woodcarving in Dongyang of Zhejiang Province are the most famous. Chaozhou woodcarving adopted multiple carving skills, such as full relief, high relief sculpture, openwork carving and others. It reveals different expressions of society with delicate artistic techniques.

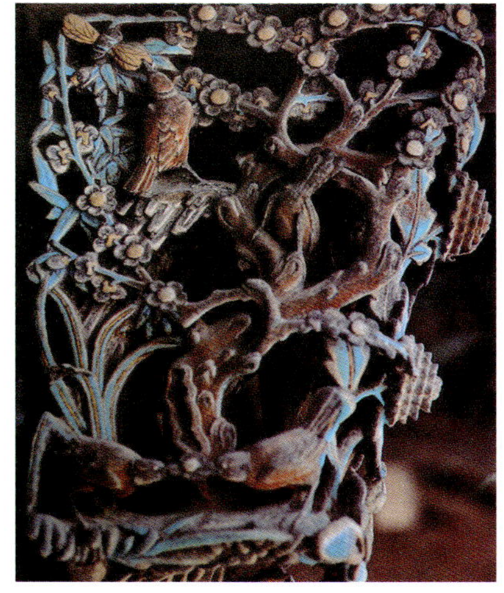

Plum blossom and bird-patterned sparrow brace of Chaozhou, Qing Dynasty.

The best brick sculptures are found at public buildings, such as memorial temples, Guandi Temples and the Temple, of the Town God. Most of these works are distributed in the southern region, especially in Guangdong, Anhui and Shanghai.

China's antique architectural sculptures underwent prominent and subtle changes over time. Each dynasty developed its own unique style. The gorgeous color of buildings has gradually faded. However, we can still recall the character of days gone by from those works that do survive.

Delight of Folk Art

Clay Figurines and Big Afu

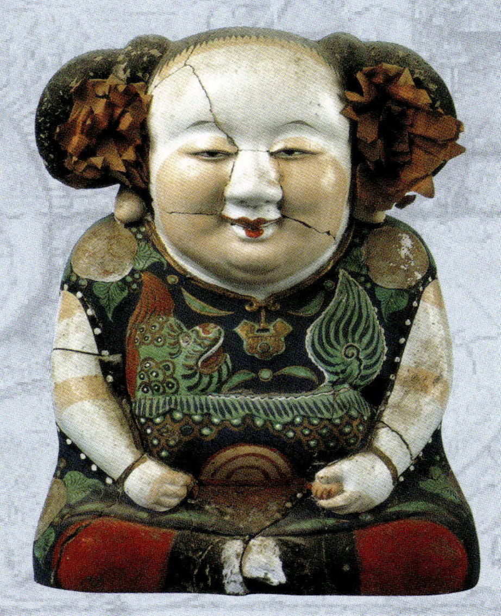

From the time of the Song Dynasty, urban economic development brought about the prosperity of folk culture, displayed in small sculptures and paintings. During the Ming and Qing dynasties, small clay sculptures with secular subjects became popular. Different from the palace carvings, folk clay sculpture represented typical folk living.

Qiaoer Muhura

Themes of children playing were common during the Song Dynasty. Paintings with hundreds of children playing and scenes of children on ceramics emerged during this dynasty. Accordingly, there were similar themes in small folk clay sculptures.

Clay babies from the time were called *Muhura* or *qiaoer*. The emergence of these small clay sculptures was directly related to folk customs from the Song Dynasty. During the Northern Song Dynasty, the Double Seventh Festival (the seventh day of the seventh lunar month) was an important day, and clay figurines were made meaning *qiqiao* ("praying for skills") so they were called *qiaoer*.

Clay figurines from the Song Dynasty were known as *Muhura*, and were closely related to the secularization of Buddhism. The Buddhist story holds that Muhura was the son of Yasodhara and Sakyamuni before he became a monk. Yasodhara was pregnant for six years and gave birth to Muhura when Sakyamuni achieved enlightenment. Later, Muhura become one of the Buddhist disciples.

About at the age of 6 or 7, Muhura brought his mother's token to visit his father. To test his credability,

Double-Seventh Festival
The seventh day of the seventh lunar month is the "Festival to Plead for Skills", which is one of the most romantic festivals in China. Zhi Nu and Niu Lang, the characters in a legend, will meet on a bridge built of magpies across the Milky Way on this evening each year. Zhi Nu is a clever, beautiful and intelligent fairy in the tale. On this night, women will plead for wisdom and skills as well as a happy marriage and intelligence, thus, the seventh day of the seventh lunar month is also known as the "Festival to Plead for Skills." Nowadays, the festival has developed into the Chinese "Valentine's Day."

Sakyamuni hid among other disciples. With innate intelligence, Muhura identified his father at first sight. It was because of this that people called this kind of clay figurine *Muhura*. People connected this story with the custom on the Seventh Day Festival, marking the origin of the tradition of displaying clay figurines during the festival. At first, the custom was prevalent in the imperial court and later became popular among the general public. At the time, imperial *Muhura* were quite luxurious; some were made with ivory, gold and jewels. However, the *Muhuras* with the greatest artistic and vitality are folk sculptures.

The making of *Muhuras* was most prevalent during the Northern Song Dynasty. *Muhura* color sculptures from the time depict a naive and fat baby holding a lotus leaf in one hand. South of the Yangtze River, Suzhou was the manufacturing center of clay figurines. Yuan Yuchang was a famous master of color sculpture, well known for his baby sculptures. It is said that he installed reed whistles in the color baby sculptures. When the babies were pressed on the head, the sculpture would give out a cry. In Lin'an (today's Hangzhou), folk color sculptures were

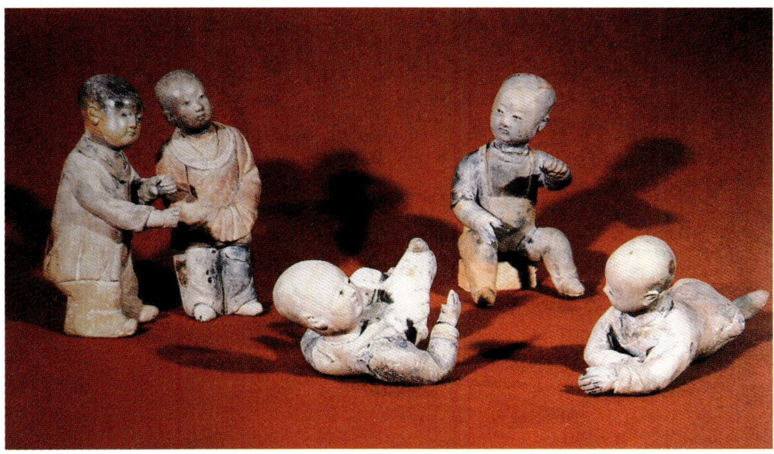

Clay boys, Song Dynasty.

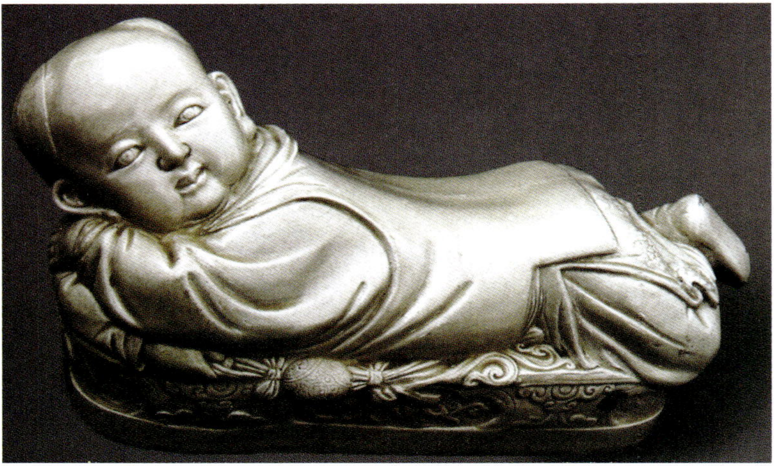

A Porcelain pillow in the shape of a child, Song Dynasty.

so prevalent that they were sold on a lane named after the clay figurines sold and where there were various small workshops specializing in making clay figurines.

In 1976, some small clay sculptures were found in one of the ruins of the Song Dynasty in Zhenjiang, Jiangsu Province. There were five complete clay figurines sculptures, about 10cm tall. The five clay figurines are similar in look, but have different postures. Without glaze, the sculptures have traces of gold dust. Most child sculptures are of portraits of boys with thin clothes, standing with their hands in their sleeves or playing.

The sculpting techniques are realistic, giving a simple and innocent feeling. These works adopted the techniques of modeling. The heads were modeled, so the five clay figurines had similar looks but the bodies gave them slight changes in position. Besides the five individual *Muhura* sculptures, a porcelain pillow in the shape of child has survived from the Song Dynasty. The work shows outstanding sculptural techniques. Its shape and look are quite similar to folk clay figurines, but are more elegant and the shape of the baby is perfectly combined with the shape of the porcelain pillow.

The appreciation of clay figurines lasted nearly five hundred years from the Song Dynasty to the Yuan Dynasty. The period also witnessed the gradual secularization of Buddhism. Advanced principles of Buddhism were skillfully combined with folk custom, and the emergence of *Muhura* sculptures is the embodiment of the secularization of Buddhism.

Playing with toys — Big Afu

From the late Ming Dynasty, the custom of making clay figurines emerged in Wuxi and became a sideline occupation for farmers. By the mid-Qing Dynasty, the custom became increasingly specialized. Special workshops with well-known folk sculptors emerged. Huishan clay sculptures are divided into rough and fine sculptures. Sculptures with made with simple techniques are rough sculptures, which became a type of toy. Fine sculptures were mostly based on traditional Chinese operas. The most famous fine sculptures are the toys called "Big Afu."

Big Afu is a clay figurine of a baby with a small animal in his arms, symbolizing good fortune, fertility and happiness. The sitting baby implies peace and harmony and gives an impression of happiness and unity. Huishan Big Afu clay figurines are usually modeled with simple structures. The technique combines painting and sculpture. In folk clay sculpture, painting is more important than the modeling itself.

For the making of Huishan clay figurines, a saying goes that technique accounts for 30% and painting 70%. Commonly used colors include green, heliotrope, ultramarine, bright red and light yellow, accompanied by a small amount of golden yellow. The details of clay figurines are outlined in black. Big Afu clay figurines from the Qing Dynasty were even more colorful with great folk decorative colors. Despite their simple structure, they give off a rich feeling.

It is said that the earliest existing Big Afu was made from an original model of the Qianlong Period of the Qing Dynasty. It is now housed in the Huishan Clay Figurine Institute. This piece of Big Afu sculpture, 22cm in height, 16.5cm in width, and 7.2cm thick, is a high relief molded clay figurine. Big Afu sits in typical clothes with his legs crossed, a full face, and holding a cyan lion in his arms, showing a strong folk style from the south Yangtze River. The look of the Big Afu is thought-provoking. Although it is an image of a baby, it shows a mature, inscrutable smile but also a simple and naive look that combines innocence and wisdom.

The image of Big Afu with a lion in his arms has the look of a conqueror, and it is a symbol of exorcism and blessing. This image is popular to this day and it is still made in Huishan.

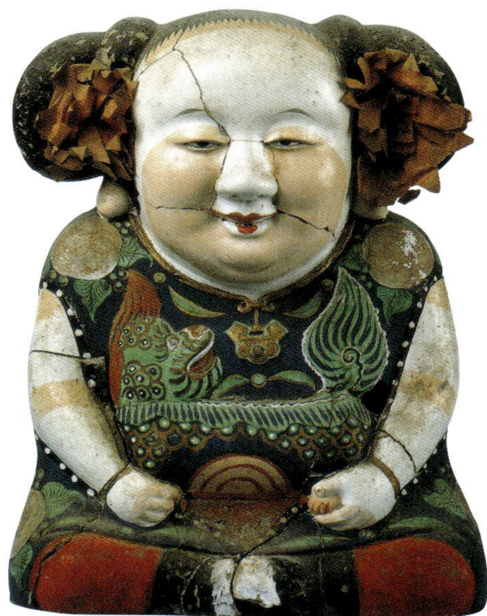

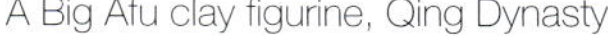

A Big Afu clay figurine, Qing Dynasty.

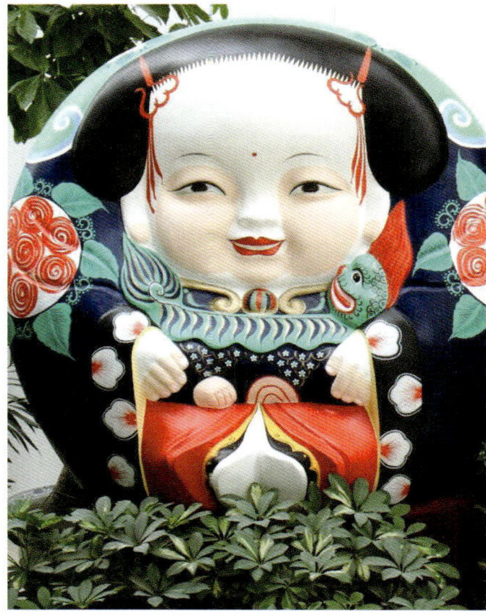

A contemporary Big Afu clay figurine.

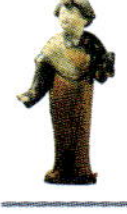

The image is now simpler and more innocent, but the symbolic meaning of blessing remains.

In 1992, the China National Tourism Administration decided to use the image of Big Afu as its mascot. In 2002, the Chinese film Golden Rooster Award and the Hundred Flowers Award took Big Afu as a mascot. Its serene and pleasant look is deeply rooted in the hearts of the Chinese people.

Hand-made figures based on traditional Chinese operas and Clay Figurine Zhang

Besides being toys, handmade figures based on traditional Chinese operas are also outstanding representatives of clay figurine art.

Hand-made figures based on traditional Chinese operas refer to clay figurines showing theatrical characters. The handmade figure is set in three major roles of a drama to reflect the plot. Later, the technique gradually began to embrace more themes, such as myths, legends, historical figures and customs. Without using molds, these handmade figurines are made by craftsmen with considerable artistic accomplishment and skill.

During the late Qing Dynasty, there was a color sculpture artist known as "Clay Figurine Zhang", Zhang Mingshan in Tianjin. Zhang was born into a family of craftsmen. He was good at making various roles from dramas and figures into reality. He was also good at forming faces and was greatly admired by people for his vivid works. Legend has it that Zhang could make vivid stage figures in his sleeves while he was watching dramas. Since Zhang had some literary accomplishments, his works are bookish and different from general folk clay works. His works were themed on the Three Kingdoms, the Story by

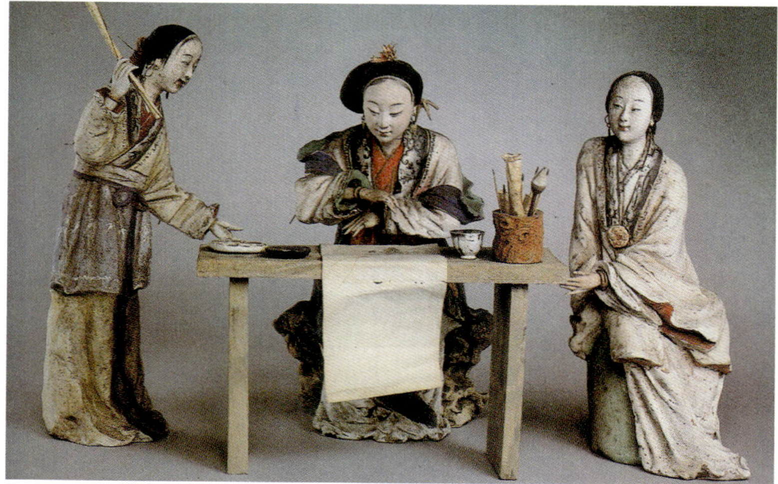

Painting Xichun, Zhang Mingshan, Qing Dynasty.

the Water Margin, and Dream of the Red Mansion. A group of works showing the Painting Xichun shows his good command of general life and elegant style. In addition, he made some works to show the joy of everyday life. The tradition of Clay Figurine Zhang continues to this day, with his successors not merely limited to the Zhang family.

Folk culture has thrived since the Song Dynasty, showing great vitality even today. Folk clay sculpture still exists in China in a relatively natural form. Cultural heritage continues in this simple and direct way.

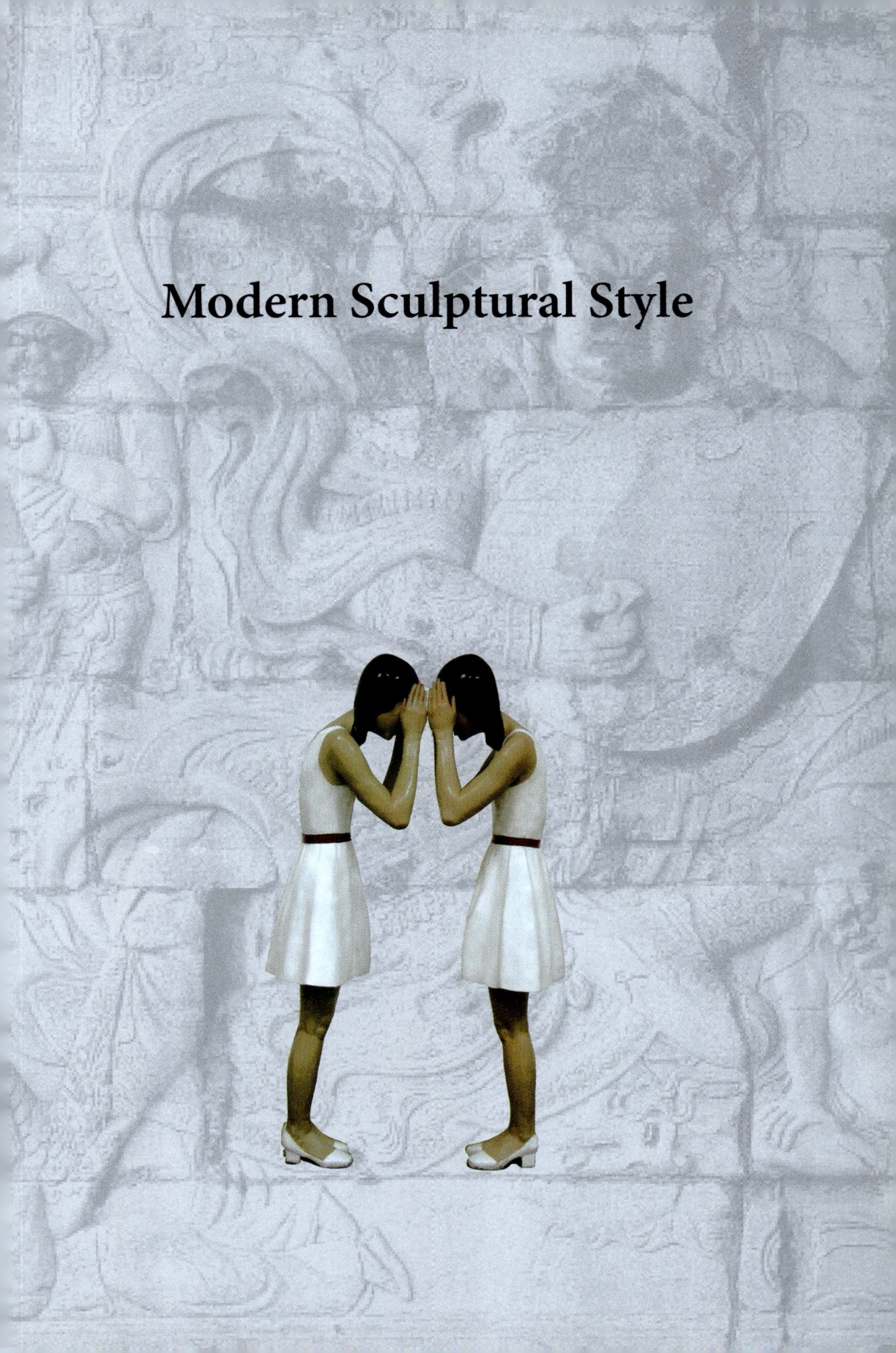

Modern Sculptural Style

The history of China's modern sculpture begins in the early twentieth century when China's centuries-old traditional sculptures lost popularity and Western style began to have an influence. At the time, Chinese intellectuals were trying to establish a new kind of culture "based on traditional Chinese values and aided with modern Western management and technology." Sculptors in the art world were also wavering between the Western system of "describing things in a strictly scientific way" and the Chinese system of "expressing the spirit by describing appearances."

The period 1949–1979 saw another phase of China's sculpture, with sculptures mainly reflecting the revolutionary ideology that prevailed in China. Shortly after the People's Republic of China was founded, Liu Kaiqu made a statue of Mao Zedong, which later became a piece of landmark artwork that signified the start of a time when sculptures expressing hero worship gained popularity. These sculptures were full of the passion typical of the revolutionary days. Many large-scale group sculptures, while designed to create a sort of optimism for the new China, satisfied ideological needs. After 1966, lots of statues of political leaders sprung up in many Chinese cities, which was a reflection of the "creation of immortals" at that particular time.

A wave of public sculptures prevailed in Chinese cities after the 1980s. Various types of sculptures were shaped among urban squares and buildings, which were amazing either in style or shape and represented different levels of sculptural art. Later, the passion for urban sculptures cooled. Since the 1990s, Chinese sculptures have experienced significant changes both in style and concept.

1911–1949: Western influence

Chinese urban sculptures began immediately after the Xinhai Revolution (1911). Outdoor sculptures were rare at that time, dominated by commemorative statues of early revolutionists. Statues of Sun Yat-sen were the most popular of all. During the 1920s and 1930s, major sculptors included Jiang Xiaojian and Li Jinfa, as well as Liu Kaiqu, a pioneer in China's modern sculpture.

Jiang Xiaojian, a Chinese artist who went to France to study sculpture in these early days, returned to embark on sculpture art in China in the 1920s. He was best known for the bronze statue of Premier Sun Yat-sen, which is now north of the government complex of Jiangwan, Shanghai. Three meters high and over ten meters tall (including the base), the sculpture integrates French-style classical carving methods, reproduces the great revolutionist in a vivid way and has become a landmark landscape in the new district of Shanghai.

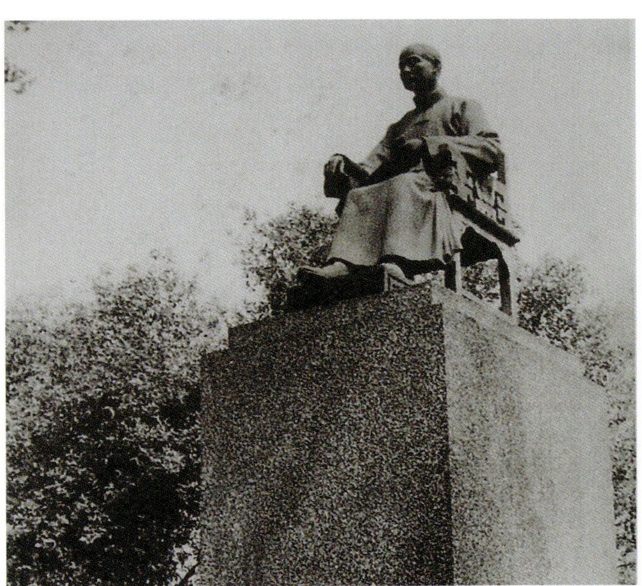

Bronze statue of Premier Sun Yat-sen, Liu Kaiqu, 1944.

Liu Kaiqu, studied fine arts in Paris. On his return to China in 1933, he taught at Hangzhou

Art College where he cultivated many sculptors for the New China. His sculpture combines classical Western techniques with traditional Chinese line-carving methods characterized by conciseness. What he sculptred presented simple, precise and exquisite styles rather than exaggerated, passionate emotions. The statue of Sun Yat-sen that he created in 1944 is now in Chunxi Road in Chengdu.

Because of the turbulence of Chinese social life in the past, very few artworks from these sculptors have been passed down. Their acute and deep insights, however, paved the way for the development of China's modern sculpture art and enrich the memories of the Chinese people.

1949–1979: From revolutionary passion to formulaic art

The introduction of sculptural methods and techniques from the West, like that of the oil paintings, was a process that saw gradual combination of the Western and Eastern cultures. Despite its rich sculpture heritage, China was deeply affected by Russian sculptural style in the 1950s, when links with the Soviet Union were widely encouraged. China's Ministry of Culture also invited Russian sculptors to set up training classes in the China Central Academy of Fine Arts in 1956, giving nationwide recruiting lectures and taking assistants in fine art schools as students.

The first big event in the sculptural history of the New China after 1949 was the establishment of the "Monument to the People's Heroes." The Chinese government decided to erect a "Monument to the People's Heroes" at Tian'anmen Square in Beijing to commemorate all the revolutionaries who fought and sacrificed for the nation's independence during 1840–1949.

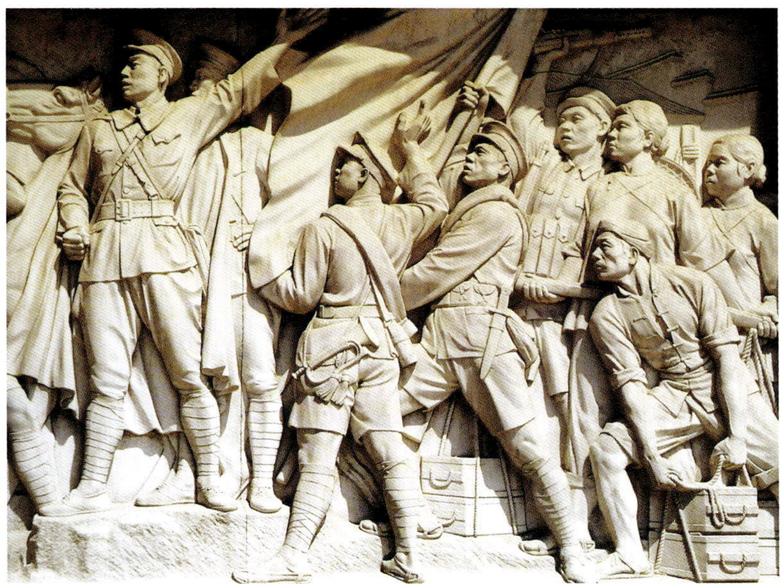

Relief on the west side of the Monument to the People's Heroes (detail), 1952.

Work on the monument formally started on August 1, 1952. Numerous Chinese artists, including sculptors and many painters, contributed to the design of the reliefs on the monument and spent four years creating the finished work. The eastern side of the relief shows the historical events of "Lin Zexu's burning of opium stocks in Humen Beach" and the "Jintian Uprising." The southern part represents the scenes in "Wuchang Uprising," "The May 4th Movement" and "The May 30th Movement." On the western side are the reliefs of the "Nanchang Uprising" and the "Anti-Japanese Guerrilla War." The northern part includes three scenes known as "Crossing the Yangtze River to Liberate the Mainland of China," "Supporting the Soldiers Engaged in the Front" and "Welcoming the People's Liberation Army." The reliefs are two meters high and 40.68m long, with about twenty heroic figures in each relief. The ten reliefs, while demonstrating the merits of every sculptor, have a relatively uniform artistic style. The majority of the artists who created the "Monument to the People's Heroes" were those returned from Europe. The overall style of the reliefs, therefore, mainly reflects Western techniques.

As well as the huge relief work of the "Monument to the People's Heroes," some important public architecture with relief work also appeared in this period. For instance, the group sculpture of "Celebrating the Harvest" created by the Lu Xun Academy of Fine Arts in 1959 received high praise from the sculptural world. Though the sculpture was intended to follow fashion, it went beyond the profound influence of the Western classical and Russian sculptural styles and demonstrated strong traditional features and cultural grandeur. That made it a "masterpiece combining both revolutionary realism and revolutionary romanticism." Concise in style, the group sculpture displayed a sense of strength that could not be checked.

The group sculpture the "Rent Collection Courtyard" was among the excellent sculptural works of the 1960s. The artwork

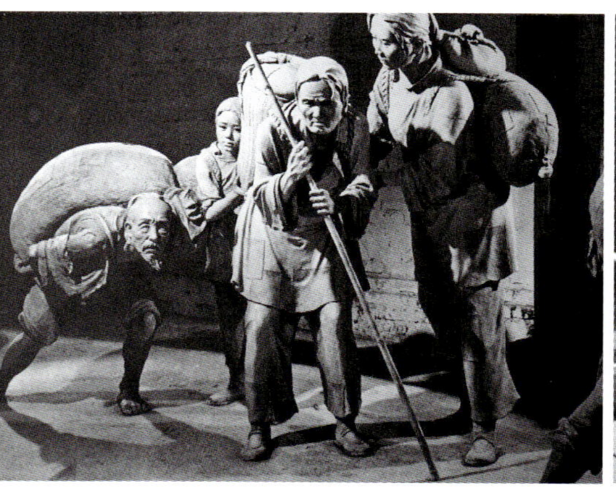

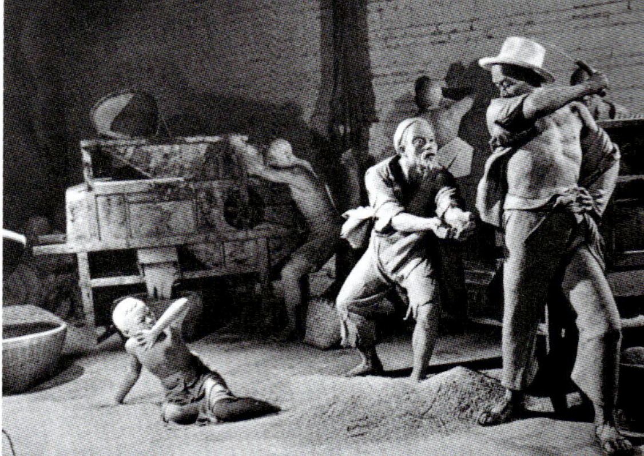

Group sculpture of Rent Collection Courtyard (detail), 1965.

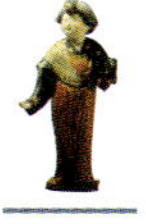

gave rise to a very interesting phenomenon in the history of sculpture in terms of the great attention it received at home and the extreme passion its audience showed, as well as in disputes arising from its use in modern art.

In June 1965, the Sichuan Academy of Fine Arts was commissioned by the CPC Sichuan Provincial Committee to create the clay sculpture of the "Rent Collection Courtyard." Teachers and students of the sculpture department quickly initiated the work, which lasted for nearly four months. The group sculpture was arranged within the fences of a rent collection courtyard, which was 118m in length and 8m in height. The contents of the sculpture included four parts—"Forced to Pay Rents," "Counting the Rents," "Press for Rents" and "Going to Fight." It involved 114 figures.

The "Rent Collection Courtyard" was quite different from average sculptures. It resembled a series of pictures more than a single sculpture for pure entertainment or a group sculpture for commemoration. It has four parts, with each part somewhat independent but subject to the theme of the sculpture with elaborately designed transitions between the parts.

Another feature of the "Rent Collection Courtyard" was the ingenious use of the courtyard as a background. This helped create a sense of reality and further gave play to the realistic style. As for the sculptural techniques, the sculptors, on one hand, expressed the traits of the sculpture based on the academic principle of art, and on the other hand, used the traditional Chinese sculptural methods for "clay Buddha" for reference and adopted straw, rough clay and fine clay mixed with cotton and sand as basic materials.

Swarms of farmers came to visit from miles away even when the work was under construction. And the group sculpture, after completion in October 1965, created a sensation in neighboring areas. The concerned authorities quickly decided to make a replica and send it to Beijing for exhibition. When part of the replica and all the pictures of the original sculpture were displayed at the National Art Gallery in Beijing on December 19, 1965, thousands of people went to visit every day. With an influence far beyond the usual boundary of art, it has won higher and higher praise.

In the 1960s, conceptual idealism began to emerge, and different techniques prevailed in the sculptural world. Some artists, still "encouraged" by excessive revolutionary enthusiasm, were extremely passionate about sculptural creation and were trying to pursue a sort of "revolutionary" beauty that was out of touch with reality. Such works became artistic forms that were formulaic, conceptual or even ridiculous, and the trend peaked in the period of the Cultural Revolution (1966-76): The "greatness" of leaders was infinitely exaggerated, and hero worship evolved into a religious fanaticism. A great many sculptures of leaders were built in an instant. Huge sculptures of Mao Zedong, who was sanctified, could be seen everywhere from urban squares and parks to transport hubs and even schools. A movement of the "creation of immortals" spread across the whole nation until the end of the Cultural Revolution.

The group sculptures on the "Monument to the People's" Heroes and the sculpture of "Rent Collection Courtyard," and the large number of formulaic sculptures that appeared afterwards, respectively represented two aspects of Chinese sculptural art in that particular historical period. The significant changes in sculptural techniques and forms reflected a big change in social ideology. Such sculptures showing great revolutionary passion gradually faded away after the 1970s and became a special memory for the Chinese people.

From 1980 to the early 21st century: Conceptual sculptural art

Since the 1980s, sculptures have been designed to be increasingly plebeian and diverse in content. Sculptors started to pay more attention to real life as well as experiences and expressions. Public art began to rise; more materials were adopted and expressive forms were diversified. In 1982, the National Urban Sculptural Planning Team and the National Urban Sculptural Art Committee led a nationwide campaign of urban sculptural creation, which indicated that China's sculptural creation had entered a new stage of official participation. The sculptors noted the lessons drawn from the Cultural Revolution, when a great many sculptures of leaders were made and the quality of art was ignored, and built a number of sculptures intended to beautify the urban environment, which included monuments and garden decorations. Urban sculptural parks of different sizes were also constructed in many cities, offering lots of works that represented art at different levels. In 1984, the Sculptural Park of Shijingshan was launched in Shijingshan District, Beijing. This was China's first sculptural park and served as a reference for the establishment of sculptural parks nationwide.

As of the middle 1980s, excellent artworks well integrated with the urban environment included:

i) The stone statue of "Fisher Girl of Zhuhai" erected on the coast in Zhuhai, Guangdong Province. Taking the images in Dunhuang frescoes for reference, the sculptors created a fisher girl who holds a shining pearl high above her head, which symbolizes the beautiful city of Zhuhai;

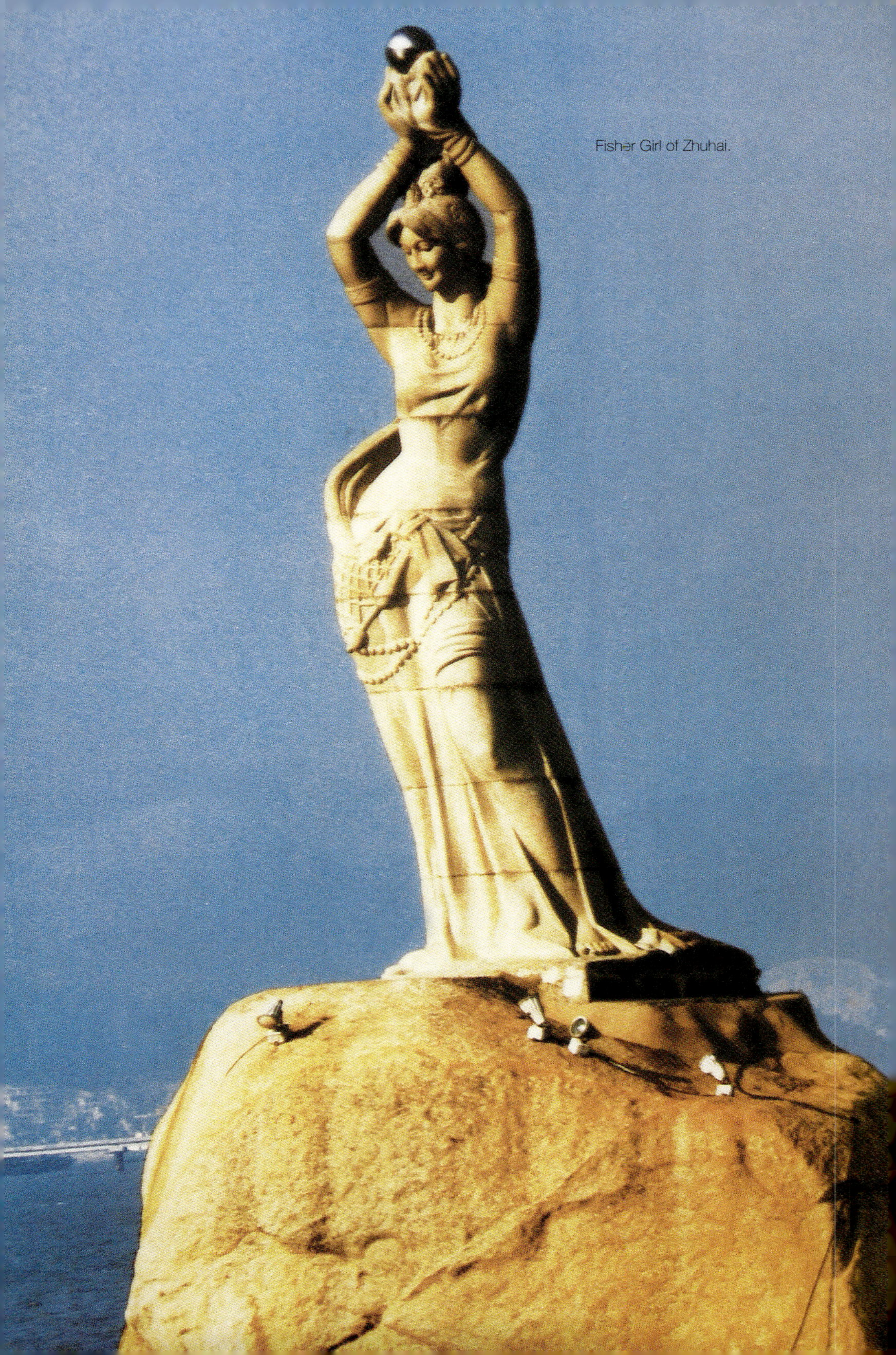

Fisher Girl of Zhuhai.

ii) The alloy group sculpture of "Spring, Summer, Autumn and Winter" placed on the end of the Yangtze River Bridge in Chongqing in 1984;
iii) The bronze sculpture of "Dove of Peace" built at Hepingli, Beijing, and the stone sculpture of "Reading" at Zhengyi Road;
iv) The stone "Fable Group Sculptures" created in Donghu Scenic Spot, Wuhan, Hubei Province;
v) The bronze sculpture of "The Willing Ox" placed in front of the complex of CPC Shenzhen Municipal Committee, which was once considered as the spiritual symbol of the emerging city and represented the pioneering spirit of the first generation of city builders. Nowadays, it has become a symbol of Shenzhen.

A "frontiers" movement initiated by young Chinese artists who advocated Western realism appeared in the middle 1980s. With the passage of time, Chinese artists, whose horizons gradually expanded, began to absorb the Western style in a more critical way, and tried to introduce Western art based on their own local culture. A contemporary Chinese historian in fine arts said, "The culture and art of any nation has its own 'feature of modern days' during its transition process from traditional forms to modern forms. China has entered a modern period since 1979, and it has its distinctive 'features of the modern days,' too...But such features of China's fine arts were different from those of other Western countries given their apparent Chinese characteristics known as 'reality.'"

From this background, most sculptors have made tentative efforts to interpret traditional sculptural languages in a new way since the 1990s, hence the presence of contemporary conceptual sculptures reflecting public awareness. The language of the artworks has become more and more novel and

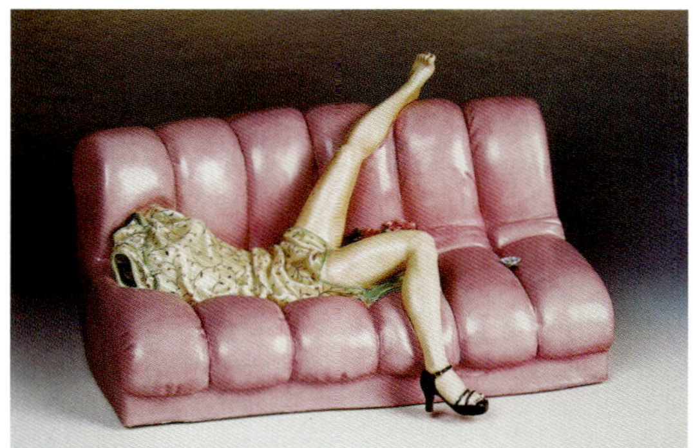

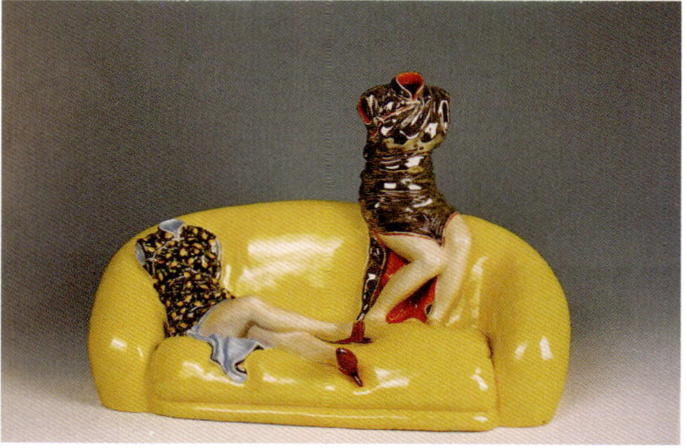

Treasureable Memory, Liu Jianhua, 1999.

pioneering, and sculptors have begun to focus more on self-reflection and self-awareness. In the meantime, a sculptural wave called "pop style" or "vulgar style" arose, which was not just limited to sculpture but also influenced many other kinds of contemporary Chinese art including painting and photography in the early 1990s. Most of the "pop" sculptors were not originally sculptors but were actually painters, represented by Liu Jianhua, Liu Liguo and Xu Yihui. The porcelain sculpture of "Treasureable Memory," created by Liu Jianhua, was among the representative artworks. He sculptured female bodies, dressed in bright Chinese traditional clothing, on colorful porcelain plates or sofas to symbolize the state of post-colonial culture and reflect the problems arising from modern consumer culture.

Since the 1990s, some contemporary sculptural artists with some international reputation have returned home, including Sui Jianguo, Li Xiangqun, Zhan Wang in Beijing, Zeng Chenggang in Zhejiang, Fu Zhongwang in Hubei as well as Huo Boyang and Wang Hongliang in Shenyang. Their sculptural works not only represent the high level of art in today's China, but also the fresh, diverse concepts manifested by contemporary Chinese sculptural art and local cultural awareness.

The influence of conceptual art on sculpture started around 1992, when the young artists like Sui Jianguo, Zhan Wang and Fu Zhongwang began to regard sculptures as carriers of conceptual art. The sculpture "Garment - Sun Yat-sen's Uniform" created by Sui Jianguo has been deeply rooted in the public mind. He expressed the "Sun Yat-sen's uniform," a kind of garment from the early revolutionary period towards which most modern Chinese feel the deepest affection, in the form of a cultural sign that was inane but could naturally be associated with the time of Mao Zedong. The sculpture reflects unique experience of Chinese history and signals the fetters that have bound the social development of modern China.

Zhan Wang is one of China's most famous contemporary sculptors. He was first known for the sculpture of "Artificial Mountain Stone," which was created in 1997. It was the first piece of contemporary Chinese sculptural work displayed by the Metropolitan Museum of Art in New York and the first piece of contemporary Chinese sculpture displayed by the De Young Museum in San Francisco. In 2008, the British Museum displayed his sculpture "Artificial Mountain Stone" among an exhibition intended to celebrate the "Year of China" as a key item of contemporary Chinese art. Zhan Wang ingeniously took the Taihu Lake stone used in classical Chinese gardens as an element for use in contemporary art. This was a conversation between time and space that demonstrated the cultural integration of modern Chinese society. As is shown in the artwork "Artificial Mountain Stone," which

Taihu Lake stone

Taihu Lake stones are materials often used in classical Chinese gardens and were first employed in royal gardens. Originally produced along the Taihu Lake close to the Dongting Mountain of Suzhou, natural Taihu Lake stones have been beaten by water waves and are thus strangely shaped with many round and deep holes. Thin, wrinkled, leaking and transparent, Taihu Lake stones demonstrate the aesthetic taste of the royal families and men of letters for traditional Chinese gardens.

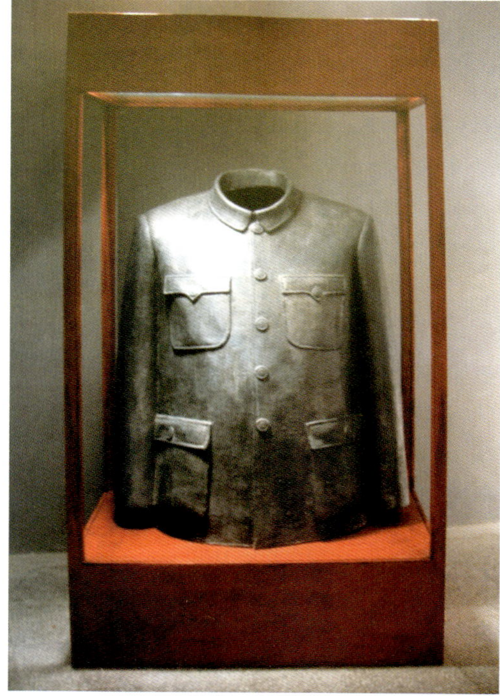
Legacy—Sun Yat-sen's Uniform, Sui Jianguo, 1998.

is made of stainless steel, traditional sculptural concepts can be dissolved and replaced by a new kind of artistic language. This accurately reflects the situation in which the traditional and modern mix together in today's China.

The works of Sui Jianguo and Zhan Wang shows the avant-garde concepts of the 1990s, which also brings contemporary Chinese sculptures into the global cultural context. Interestingly, the sculptors who preferred creation of very modern art in the early 1990s, such as Sui Jianguo, began returning to traditional sculpture forms in the late 1990s. Since the twenty-first century the themes found in contemporary Chinese sculptures have been further enriched, including post-colonialism, feminism, criticisms about social consumption and the practice of neo-historicism.

The representative of feminism is Xiang Jing, whose work highlights painting as a form of sculptural language. She uses female sculptures to describe society and the sense of nihilism that commonly exists. Yu Fan is among the representatives of neo-historicism. By creating historical figures, he brings the audience

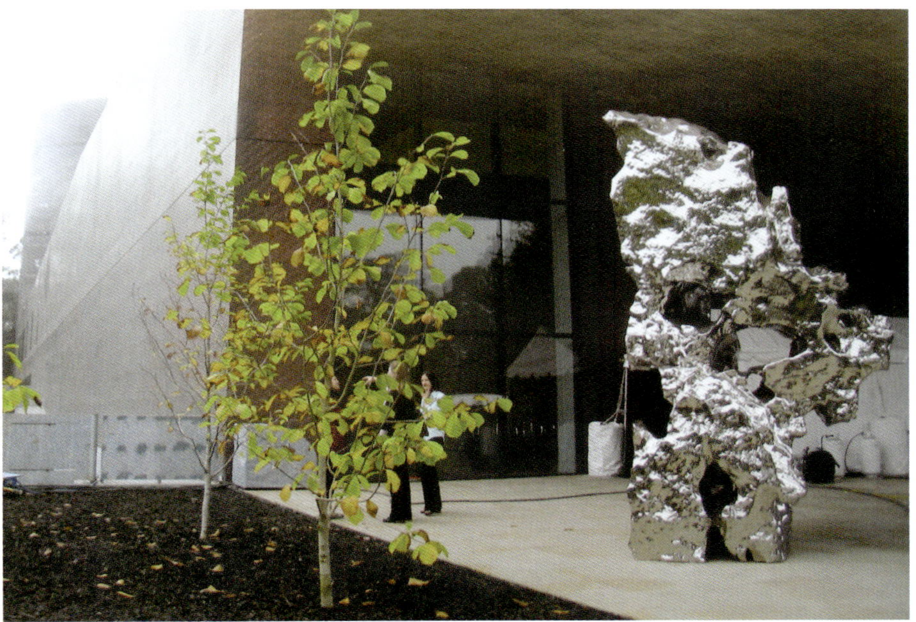

Artificial mountain stone, Zhan Wang, 1997.

back to the history that the sculptural images belong to. His sculpture of the revolutionary martyr Liu Hulan is an example.

China's sculptures have undergone different stages of evolution over the past 20–30 years - from the enthusiasm for modernism in the 1980s, to calm pondering on post-modern diversity in the 1990s and an even more mature attitude adopted today, with global vision further broadened. This maturity reflects the growth of certain strength in contemporary Chinese culture.

Over the past century, China's sculptures have absorbed and integrated the sculptural styles and techniques of the West. Meanwhile, Chinese sculptors are also trying to seek a style and concepts that truly belong to the Chinese people. Influenced by contemporary art, China's sculptures grow more and more mature, focusing on humanity and social issues and global issues.

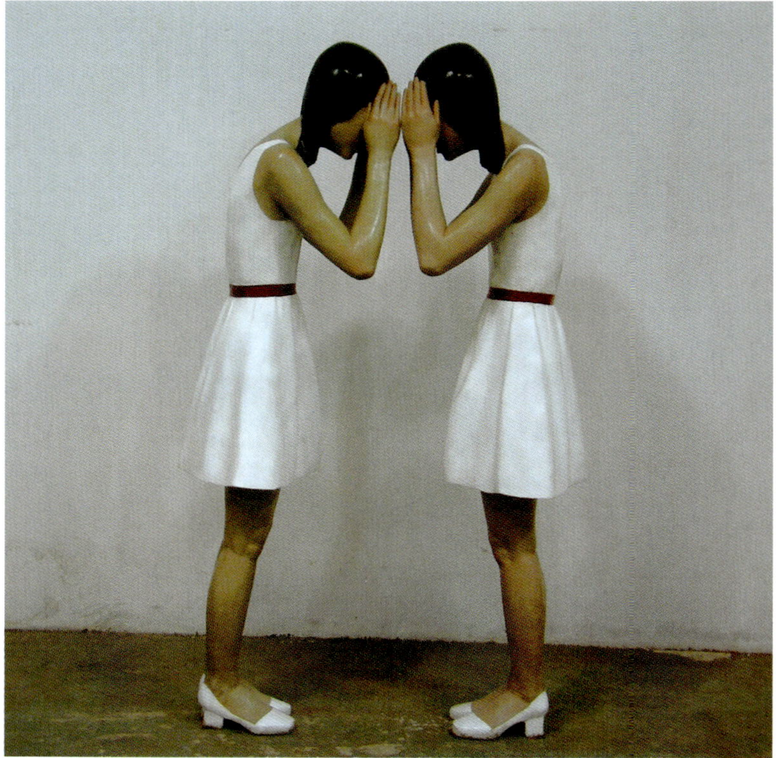

The End, Xiang Jing, 2000.

These artworks, designed to be more open in both style and content, can serve as a bridge for communication between the East and West. The efforts of artists today encourage the world to understand Chinese culture and China's current situation.

Appendix: Chronological Table of the Chinese Dynasties

The Paleolithic Period	c.1,700,000–10,000 years ago
The Neolithic Period	c. 10,000–4,000 years ago
Xia Dynasty	2070–1600 BC
Shang Dynasty	1600–1046 BC
Western Zhou Dynasty	1046–771 BC
Spring and Autumn Period	770–476 BC
Warring States Period	475–221 BC
Qin Dynasty	221–206 BC
Western Han Dynasty	206 BC–AD 25
Eastern Han Dynasty	25–220
Three Kingdoms	220–280
Western Jin Dynasty	265–317
Eastern Jin Dynasty	317–420
Northern and Southern Dynasties	420–589
Sui Dynasty	581–618
Tang Dynasty	618–907
Five Dynasties	907–960
Northern Song Dynasty	960–1127
Southern Song Dynasty	1127–1276
Yuan Dynasty	1276–1368
Ming Dynasty	1368–1644
Qing Dynasty	1644–1911
Republic of China	1912–1949
People's Republic of China	Founded in 1949